Home Woodworking & Finishing

Complete Handyman's Library™
Handyman Club of America
Minneapolis, Minnesota

Published in 1995 by
Handyman Club of America
12301 Whitewater Drive
Minnetonka, Minnesota 55343

Published by arrangement with Cy DeCosse Incorporated
ISBN 0-86573-746-0

Printed on American paper by
R. R. Donnelley & Sons Co.
99 98 97 96 / 5 4 3 2

CREDITS:
Created by: The Editors of Cy DeCosse Incorporated
and the staff of the Handyman Club of America
in cooperation with Black & Decker. **BLACK&DECKER®**
is a trademark of Black & Decker (US), Incorporated
and is used under license.

Handyman Club of America:
    Book Marketing Manager: Cal Franklin
    Book Marketing Coordinator: Jay McNaughton

Contents

Introduction

Home Woodworking & Finishing is just the book you need to build any woodworking project you wish to make. From basic woodworking techniques to creating a fine finish, you'll find everything you need to know to produce creative and outstanding projects. And the step-by-step photographs and instructions will help you do the best possible work.

First, the Project Preview section shows you many design possibilities for built-in projects for your home. The options shown here also will give you ideas for other woodworking projects.

The following section, Built-in Basics, provides all the information necessary to choose the right materials, tools and accessories, and fasteners for your work. You also learn how to plan your project and prepare the project site. Then basic techniques are shown for making a variety of essential joints and adding shelves, doors, drawers, and electrical accessories that will help you build any project.

Built-in Projects presents plans, cutting lists, and step-by-step instructions for building ten unique built-in projects. You also see how to adapt these plans to match your specific requirements. From floor-to-ceiling shelves and basic cabinets to an entertainment center, you will find many exciting possibilities for adding to the usefulness, value, and appeal of your home.

To help you complete any of your woodworking projects, the Finishing section shows you how to apply an excellent finish. You learn the basics of selecting a finish, preparing wood surfaces prior to finishing, and the specific methods for applying various coloring agents, paints, and topcoats. You

also find out how to work safely with these chemicals and properly clean up and dispose of them when you have completed your project.

Home Woodworking & Finishing will help you build many beautiful and functional woodworking projects for your home. In addition, the information you'll find here will provide you with many satisfying hours spent in the joys of woodworking and finishing.

NOTICE TO READERS

This book provides useful instructions, but we cannot anticipate all of your working conditions or the characteristics of your materials and tools. For safety, you should use caution, care, and good judgment when following the procedures described in this book. Consider your own skill level and the instructions and safety precautions associated with the various tools and materials shown. Neither the publisher nor Black & Decker® can assume responsibility for any damage to property or injury to persons as a result of misuse of the information provided.

The instructions in this book conform to "The Uniform Plumbing Code," "The National Electrical Code Reference Book," and "The Uniform Building Code" current at the time of its original publication. Consult your local Building Department for information on building permits, codes, and other laws as they apply to your project.

Project Preview

As you will see on the following pages, built-in projects provide useful storage while giving your home unique visual appeal. The featured projects range from simple wall cabinets to large built-ins that define the look and feel of an entire room. Some can be built in a few hours, while others may require a long weekend.

Each project can be built using a wide variety of materials, and the designs themselves were created so they can be adapted easily to fit unique spaces or special uses. Project variations are limited only by your creativity.

Built-ins become permanent features of your home, so plan carefully to ensure that your projects make efficient use of space and adequately meet the needs of your life-style. When choosing a location for a built-in, look for wall or floor spaces with unusual sizes or shapes, or areas that see little day-to-day use. By taking advantage of wasted space, a well-planned built-in can make a room seem larger. Built-ins that are recessed into wall spaces are especially effective because they add organized storage areas without using up valuable floor space.

A well-planned built-in project uses design details and building materials that complement the overall look of your home. Always try to make your project look like it was part of the original home plan—not an afterthought. Built-ins that are well designed and carefully constructed make your home more useful for you, more attractive to visitors, and more appealing to potential buyers.

Entertainment center (pages 114 to 123) organizes and stores bulky electronic equipment. It has a hardwood face frame, with cabinet doors and drawers that hide the equipment when it is not in use. This entertainment center features a modular center unit and two end units that are built separately. The overall width of the entertainment center, as shown, is 6 ft., 8". The project can be adapted easily by building additional end units.

Project Preview

Kneewall cabinet (pages 56 to 61) makes productive use of the low wall space found under a slanted roof line. For more extensive storage, position several cabinets side-by-side. **A:** Make an efficient, simple entertainment center by fitting the kneewall cabinet with shelves, cabinet doors, and electrical receptacles. **B:** Create space-saving storage shelves for toys, games, or books. **C:** Make a clothes dresser by adding drawers to the knee-wall cabinet.

Recessed wall shelves (pages 52 to 55) fit inside the space between wall studs. **A:** Create a small game or storage cabinet by adding doors. **B:** Create a pass-through between rooms by opening the wall from both sides and installing a wide shelf. **C:** Make a decorative display by adding several open shelves.

Floor-to-ceiling shelves
(pages 66 to 71) are con-
structed with stationary middle
shelves for strength, and adjustable shelves for flexible
storage. **A:** Create a home
library in any room by covering a wall with floor-to-ceiling
shelves. **B:** Highlight decorative collectibles by adding low-
voltage fixtures (page 48) to
the bottom sides of shelves.

Platform bench (pages 72 to 79) is a unique built-in with old-style charm. **A:** Make an indoor potting surface for plants by topping the bench with water-resistant ceramic tile. Keep planting supplies inside the bench. **B:** Create open storage for keeping quilts, decorative items, or oversized books. **C:** Build a traditional window seat by adding seat cushions and cabinet doors.

Project Preview

Basic wall cabinet and base cabinet (pages 86 to 95) feature a simple, universal design used by professional cabinetmakers. Basic cabinets can be adapted to a variety of uses, and work well in almost any room. **A:** Create utility cabinets for a laundry room, basement, or garage by building basic cabinets using inexpensive pine face frames and plywood panels. Finish the cabinets with enamel paint. **B:** Make a decorative hutch for a dining room or living room by building the cabinets from quality hardwood materials, and installing custom-made glass doors.

A

B

Corner cabinet (pages 80 to 85) provides ample storage by making good use of empty corner space. **A:** Add a unique bedroom wardrobe by building the corner cabinet with extra shelves and cabinet doors. **B:** Make a computer work center by equipping the corner cabinet with electrical receptacles and low-voltage lights.

Room divider (pages 104 to 113) separates a room into two living areas. **A:** Make an informal dining area by building a room divider next to the kitchen area and installing a wide countertop to provide an eating surface. **B:** Create a home study by using a room divider to isolate a small portion of a room.

A

B

Project Preview

Understairs work center (pages 96 to 103) makes use of the triangular space underneath a stairway—an area that is wasted space in most homes. **A:** Make a space-saving home office with a wide desktop and plenty of storage for supplies. **B:** Create a snack center for a recreation room by adding a ceramic countertop, a microwave oven, and a small refrigerator.

14

Utility shelving (pages 62 to 65) is a simple built-in that provides versatile storage for any unfinished space or informal living area. **A:** Store recycling containers and oversized lawn and garden supplies in a garage or shed. **B:** Raise workshop tools and camping equipment away from damp basement floors. **C**: Dress up utility shelves for family room storage by adding side panels and a face frame. Face frame pieces can be unscrewed and removed to rearrange shelves.

Built-In Basics

Materials

Built-in projects can vary considerably in size and style, but most can be constructed with materials available at any home improvement center. In some cases, you may need to visit a woodworker's supply store or large wholesale lumber yard to find unique woods, unusual moldings, or specialty hardware items.

To save money, construct your built-ins using finish-grade plywood for the main body (carcass), then trim exposed areas with more costly solid woods and moldings.

Lumber: Redwood (A) and cedar (B) are warm-colored softwoods used for exposed surfaces of a built-in. Because of their attractive color and grain, they usually are left unfinished or coated with a clear finish. Pine (C) is an easy-to-cut softwood often used for built-ins that will be painted. Framing lumber (D) includes rough grades of softwood pine and fir. It is used for structural framing and utility shelving. Poplar (E), a light-colored hardwood with very straight grain, is an excellent wood for fine painted surfaces. Maple (F) and oak (G) are heavy, strong hardwoods with attractive grain patterns. They usually are finished with tinted oils or stains.

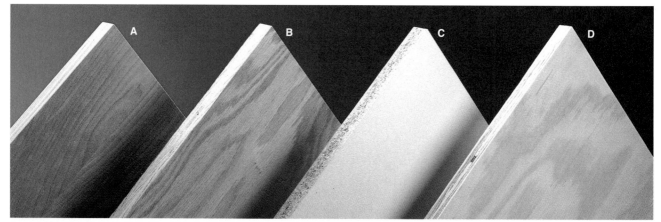

Sheet goods: Finish-grade plywood, including birch plywood (A) and oak plywood (B) are made from several layers of softwood veneer sandwiched between hardwood surface veneers. Finish-grade plywoods are used for exposed areas of a built-in, and usually are edged with hardwood strips or moldings. Birch plywood frequently is used for surfaces that will be painted, and oak plywood is usually finished with tinted oils or stains. Particleboard (C), coated with a plastic resin called melamine, is used for making contemporary-style built-ins. Sanded pine plywood (D) is a good material for built-ins that will be painted, or for hidden areas. **NOTE:** Most sheet goods are sold in 4 ft. × 8 ft. sheets, in 1/4", 1/2", or 3/4" thicknesses; some types also are sold in 2 ft. × 4 ft. and 4 ft. × 4 ft. sheets.

Trim moldings are both decorative and functional. They can be used to cover gaps around the base and sides of a built-in, to hide the edges of plywood surfaces, or simply to add visual interest to the project. Moldings are available in dozens of styles, but the samples shown here are widely available at all home improvement centers.

Synthetic trim moldings, available in many styles, are less expensive than hardwood moldings. Synthetic moldings are made of wood composites (A) or rigid foam (B) covered with a layer of melamine.

Baseboard molding (C) is used to trim the bottom edge of a built-in along the floor line. Choosing molding that matches the baseboard used elsewhere in your home gives your project a natural, built-in look.

Hardwood strips (D) are used to construct face frames for a built-in, and to cover unfinished edges of plywood shelves. Maple, oak, and poplar strips are widely available in 1 × 2, 1 × 3, and 1 × 4 sizes.

Crown moldings (E, F) cover gaps between the top of a built-in and the ceiling. Crown molding also adds a decorative accent to a built-in.

Cove molding (G) is a simple, unobtrusive trim for covering gaps between a built-in project and a wall or ceiling.

Ornamental moldings, including spindle-and-rail (H) and embossed moldings (I, J), give a built-in a distinctive decorative look.

Door-edge molding (K), sometimes called cap molding, is used with finish-grade plywood to create panel-style doors and drawer faces.

Shelf-edge molding (L), sometimes called base cap molding, gives a decorative edge to plywood shelves.

Base shoe molding (M) covers gaps around the top, bottom, and sides of a built-in. Because it bends easily, base shoe molding works well to cover irregular gaps caused by uneven walls and floors.

Power tools used for constructing built-ins include: power miter saw (A), circular saw with general-purpose and hollow-ground blades (B), router with straight bits and decorative bits (C), power screw-driver (D), pad sander (E), jig saw with wood-cutting blades (F), belt sander (G), reciprocating saw (H), and drill with brad-point and forstner bits (I).

Tools & Fasteners

Most built-in projects can be constructed using ordinary hand and power tools you may already own. A large stationary tool, like a table saw, can be useful for a few tasks, but most projects in this book are designed so they can be built with simple tools and materials.

A well-constructed built-in project depends on accurate measuring, cutting, and fastening. Unless you have considerable experience, it is a good idea to practice your skills on scrap materials before starting a project.

A table saw is a good tool for making long rip cuts and bevel cuts. Table saws are available at some rental centers.

Hand tools you may need include: bar clamps (A), handsaw (B), level (C), framing square (D), wood mallet (E), handscrew clamps (F), putty knife (G), screwdrivers (H), hammer (I), chisel (J), paintbrush (K), marking gauge (L), tape measure (M), nail set (N), C-clamps (O), compass (P), utility knife (Q), plumb bob (R), stud finder (S), pencil (T), combination square (U), and hand sander (V).

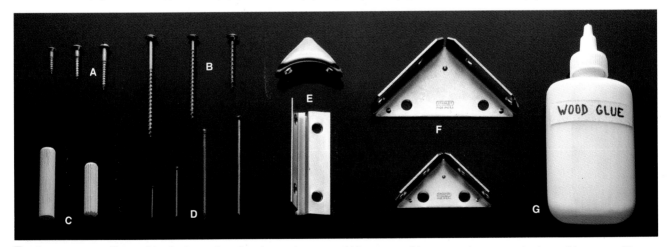

Fasteners you will need include: galvanized wood screws (A), power-driver wood screws designed for use with power screwdrivers (B), wood dowels (C), finish nails (D), metal corner brackets (E), countertop brackets (F), and wood glue (G).

Tool Accessories

A portable clamping bench, like the Workmate®, can be moved easily to your work site to provide a convenient work surface. The Workmate has a jointed, adjustable table that tightens to clamp workpieces securely. Bench stops and horizontal clamps fit into openings in the bench surface, and adapt the Workmate to many uses.

A few tool accessories, some purchased and some made yourself, will help you work more accurately and quickly when constructing a built-in.

A straightedge guide like the one shown on the opposite page can be adapted to help you make perfectly straight cuts with a router, circular saw, or jig saw. The length of your straightedge guide depends on the size of the workpieces you will be cutting. Many do-it-yourselfers make straightedge guides in 2-ft., 4-ft., and 8-ft. lengths for convenience.

Dowel jig holds workpieces to ensure that drilled dowel holes will line up properly. (See page 34.)

Right-angle drill guide attached to a drill helps bore straight holes. The bit stop mounted on the guide lets you bore holes to an accurate and uniform depth.

Adjustable router edge guide attaches to the base of your router and helps make straight dado grooves within 6" of the edge of a workpiece.

1 Mark a straight, even line lengthwise onto a 10"-wide strip of ¼" finish-grade plywood, about 4" from the edge. Cut a straight 1 × 2 cleat to the same length as the plywood strip.

2 Apply wood glue to the bottom of the cleat, then position it with one edge along the marked line on the plywood. Clamp one end of the cleat to the plywood, then add more clamps every 12", bending the cleat, if necessary, to follow the line. Let the glue dry, then remove the clamps.

Straightedge guide for a router: Create the proper setback by cutting off excess plywood with a router and straight bit, holding the base of the router firmly against the cleat. Make sure to cut with the same size bit you will be using in your projects; if you will be using more than one bit, make a separate straightedge guide for each. (To use the straightedge guide, follow the technique shown on page 118.)

Straightedge guide for a circular saw: Create the proper setback by cutting off excess plywood with a circular saw. (To use the straightedge guide, follow the technique shown on page 118.)

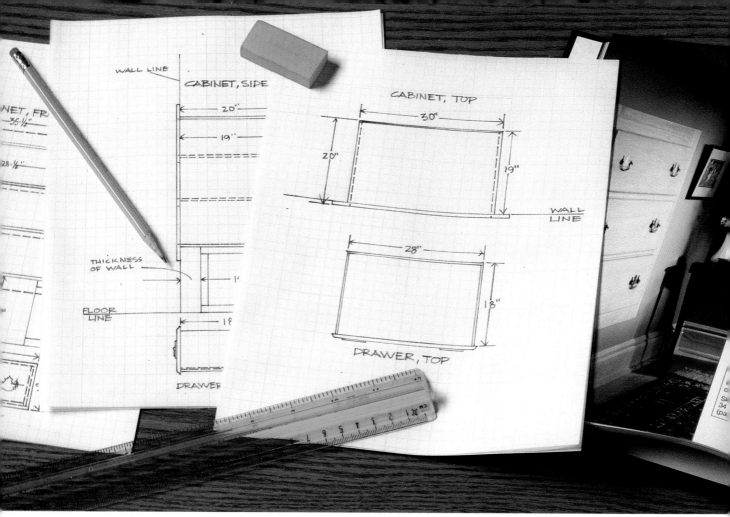

Make accurate scaled drawings on graph paper when adapting one of the built-in projects featured in this book. Use a simple scale, like 1 square = 1", to draw a side, top, and one or more front views of your project. For a complicated project, draw several front views showing the basic walls (carcass) of the built-in, the face frame construction, and the finished project including drawers and doors. Side views and top views should show all trim pieces and moldings. Make sure to use the actual measurements of sheet goods and dimension lumber when making your drawings.

Planning a Built-In Project

With each of the ten built-in projects found in this book, you can either build the project as shown, or adapt the design to fit your unique spaces and needs. To build the project as shown, follow the measurements in the parts table that accompanies each project. Small width and height adjustments can be made using the fitting tips on page 26.

In some cases, however, you may want to adapt a project design to create a larger or smaller built-in. If so, use the column of empty spaces next to the parts table to fill in your own measurements.

When adapting a built-in design, it is very important to make accurate plan drawings on graph paper to show how the project will fit in your space. These drawings let you organize your work and find approximate measurements for parts; they also make it easier to estimate the cost of materials.

To ensure a professional look and functional use, plan your built-ins so they fall within the standard range of sizes used by cabinet makers and furniture manufacturers (page opposite.)

Whether you are adapting a project or following a design as shown, it is safer to measure and cut the pieces as you assemble the built-in in its location, rather than to precut all pieces in advance. Small discrepancies in marking, cutting, and assembly techniques can lead to costly errors if you precut all the pieces.

Standard Built-in Measurements

Highest shelf should be no more than 80" above the floor to be within easy reach.

Shelves should be at least 10" deep in bookcases, and 12" deep in hanging wall cabinets. Space the shelves so there is at least 1 1/2" of open space above the items you are storing.

First shelf in a wall-hung built-in should be at least 18" above a countertop.

Work-surface height varies depending on how the surface is used. Place the surface 24" above the floor for a typing desk or sewing work center. Place the countertop at 36" for standard kitchen cabinets, and at 44" for a dry bar or eating counter.

Standard seating surfaces, like window seats and desk chairs, are between 16" and 20" high.

Base cabinet depth varies from 15" for a room divider to 30" for cabinets that support a desk surface. Standard kitchen-style floor cabinets usually are 24" or 25" in depth.

Access space in front of a built-in should be at least 36" to provide kneeling space for opening drawers and cabinet doors.

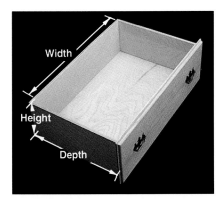

Drawer sizes range from a minimum of 3" high, 8" wide, and 8" deep; to a maximum of 10" high, 36" wide, and 30" deep. Large drawers, more than 24" wide, should be equipped with two drawer slides for stability.

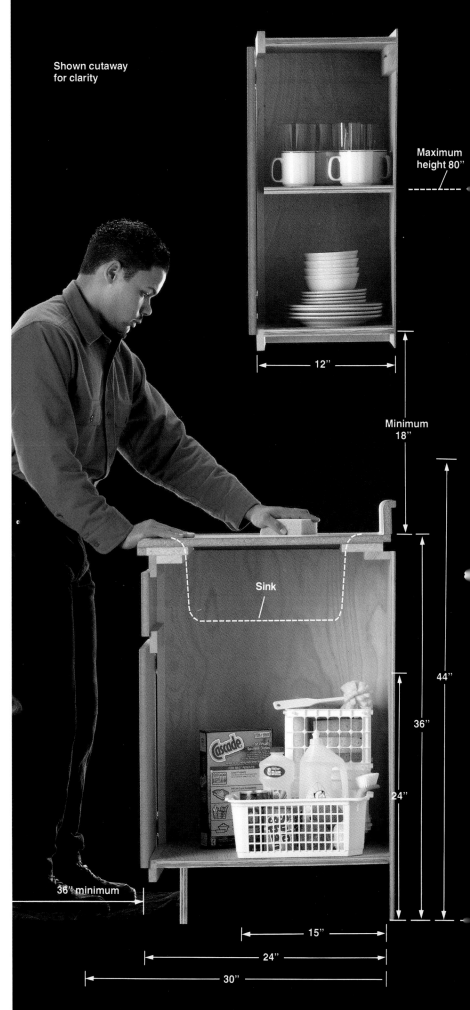

Fitting Tips for Built-ins

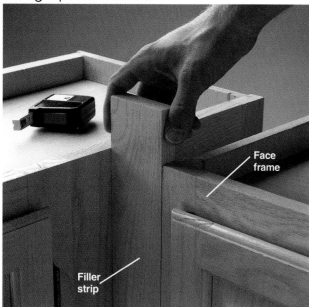

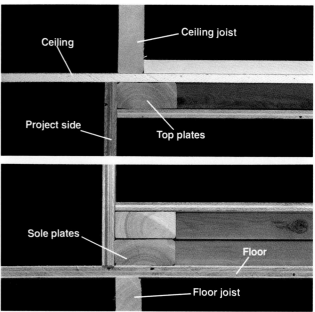

Make small width adjustments (up to 6" on each side) with hardwood strips measured and cut to fill the extra space. Attach the strips to the edges of the face frame with counterbored wood screws. These "filler strips" let you slightly enlarge a project without making changes to the basic design. Filler strips also can be scribed to fit uneven walls.

Make small height adjustments by changing the thickness of the sole plates or top plates that anchor the built-in to the floor and ceiling. The floor-to-ceiling projects in this book are designed to fit rooms with 8-ft. ceilings. If your room height differs slightly, adjusting the sole plates or top plates lets you adapt a project without major design changes.

Tips for Planning a Built-in Project

Nominal size	Actual size
1 × 2	3/4" × 1 1/2"
1 × 3	3/4" × 2 1/2"
1 × 4	3/4" × 3 1/2"
1 × 6	3/4" × 5 1/2"
1 × 8	3/4" × 7 1/4"
2 × 4	1 1/2" × 3 1/2"
2 × 6	1 1/2" × 5 1/2"
2 × 8	1 1/2" × 7 1/4"
2 × 10	1 1/2" × 9 1/4"

Measure spaces carefully. Floors, walls, and ceilings are not always level or plumb, so measure at several points. If measurements vary from point-to-point, use the shortest measurement to determine the height or width of your built-in.

Measure your materials. Actual thickness for plywood can vary from the listed nominal size; 3/4" plywood, for example, can vary in thickness by nearly 1/8".

Use actual measurements, not nominal measurements, of dimension lumber when planning a built-in. Table above shows the actual dimensions of common lumber.

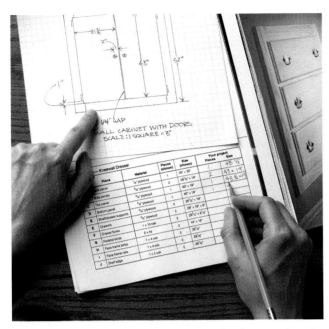

Revise the listed measurements of a featured project, if necessary, and write them down in the blank spaces found in the Parts List provided with each project. Use your scaled drawings as a guide for estimating the revised measurements. Always double-check measurements before cutting pieces to prevent costly cutting errors.

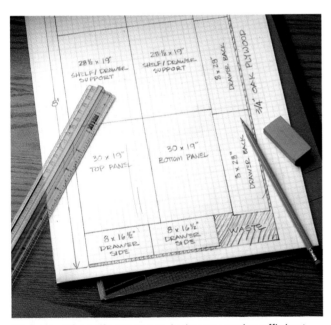

Make cutting diagrams to help you make efficient use of materials. Make scale drawings of sheet goods on graph paper, and sketch cutting lines for each part of your project. When laying out cutting lines, remember that the cutting path (kerf) of a saw blade can consume up to 1/8" of wood.

Materials	Amount needed	Cost for each	Total cost
Plywood (4 ft. × 8 ft.)			
1/4" sheets			
1/2" sheets			
3/4" sheets			
Lumber			
1 × 2 boards			
1 × 3 boards			
1 × 4 boards			
1 × 6 boards			
1 × 8 boards			
2 × 4s			
Moldings			
Door-edge			
Shelf-edge			
Base shoe			
Baseboard			
Crown/cove			
Ornamental			
Hardware			
Finish nails			
Power-driver screws			
Angle brackets			
Countertop brackets			
Drawer slides			
Hinges			
Door latches			
Pulls/knobs			
Other materials			
Wood glue			
Oil/stain			
Sanding sealer			
Paint			
Outlet strips			
Grommets			
Light fixtures			
Total cost:			$

Make a list of materials, using your plan drawings and cutting diagrams as a guide. Photocopy this materials list, and use it to organize your work and estimate costs.

Use a cardboard template or a tape outline to mark the planned location of your built-in in the work area. If you discover that room corners are not square or that walls are uneven, you will need to purchase trim pieces, like base shoe or cove moldings, to cover gaps between the walls and your built-in project.

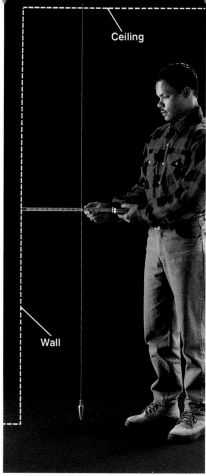

Identify bowed, irregular walls by hanging a plumb bob from the ceiling near the work area and measuring between the string and the wall at several points. Mark wall where distance is shortest; the built-in should be constructed so the back is plumb and flush at this point.

Preparing the Work Area

Before beginning a built-in project, take time to carefully evaluate and prepare your work area. Good preparation simplifies your work and ensures professional-looking results.

Locate and mark framing members in the project area so you can anchor your built-in securely. Where necessary, remove trim moldings and carpeting so the built-in will fit flush against walls. If a project will require you to cut into walls, pinpoint the location of electrical wires, plumbing pipes, and heating ducts before you begin.

Evaluate the walls and floor in the project area to see if they are square and straight. A common mistake made by many do-it-yourselfers is to alter a project design in an effort to make it fit irregular corners or walls that are badly out of plumb. Build your project so it is square, level, and plumb; then buy trim moldings to cover any gaps caused by leaning walls or sloping floors.

Locate studs and ceiling joists using an electronic stud finder. When passed over a plaster or wallboard surface, the stud finder pinpoints the edges of framing members by sensing changes in density.

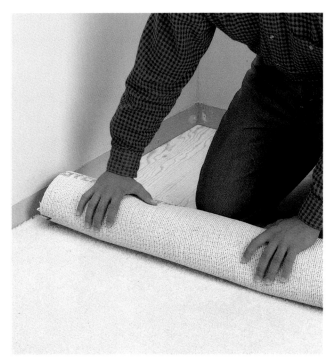

Detach and roll back carpeting and pad before beginning construction, then trim to fit around the built-in after work is completed. Jute-back carpeting must be restretched and attached to new tackless strips. **NOTE:** If you have glued-down carpeting, it may be easier to install the built-in on top of the carpeting without removing it.

Remove baseboards and other moldings to make room for a built-in that will fit flush against a wall. Use a flat pry bar with a wood block to prevent damage to the wall, and pry carefully to avoid splintering the molding. After the built-in is installed, cut the molding to size, and reattach it.

Move electrical receptacles and other fixtures, if they are in the way of your planned built-in. You also may need to add receptacles for an entertainment center or other projects that require electrical service. **NOTE:** If you are not experienced at working with wiring, hire an electrician to do this work.

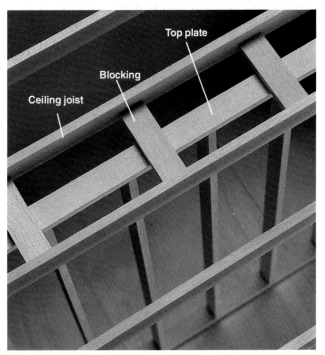

Top plate

Blocking

Ceiling joist

Install blocking between joists or studs to provide a solid surface for anchoring a built-in that does not line up with existing framing members. A room divider, for example, may require blocking between ceiling joists so it can be anchored to the ceiling.

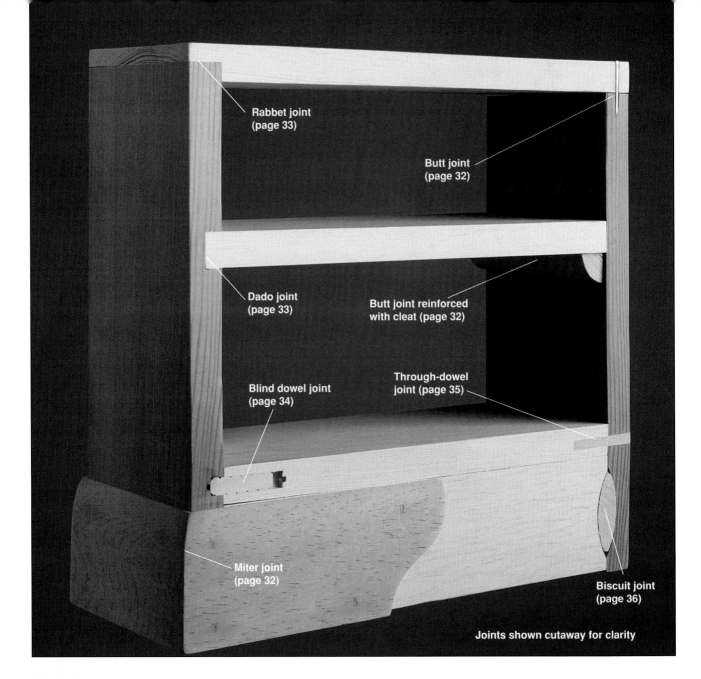

Rabbet joint
(page 33)

Butt joint
(page 32)

Dado joint
(page 33)

Butt joint reinforced
with cleat (page 32)

Through-dowel
joint (page 35)

Blind dowel joint
(page 34)

Miter joint
(page 32)

Biscuit joint
(page 36)

Joints shown cutaway for clarity

Making Joints

Joinery—the technique of creating strong, durable joints between separate pieces of wood—is essential to a successful built-in. Professional cabinet makers use dozens of joinery techniques, but a few simple joints shown on the following pages are all you need to construct the built-in projects featured in this book.

The joinery methods you choose depend on how the built-in will be used, and on the desired look. For example, a built-in used to display small items, like decorative glassware, can be made with simple butt joints reinforced with glue and finish nails. But a project that will hold heavy items, like a set of encyclopedias, should

be made with solid dado joints reinforced with screws. If appearance is very important, choose joinery techniques that conceal the methods of connection. For example, a built-in project constructed with blind dowel joints or biscuit joints has a more professional look than one made with cleated butt joints.

For many built-ins, you will need to glue and clamp several joints at the same time—a job that requires a number and variety of clamps (page 21). For maximum strength and durability, use wood glue to reinforce all joints. Joints made with nails or screws alone are more likely to loosen over time.

Basic Gluing Techniques

Clean surfaces that will be glued, using a lint-free cloth. Smooth off any rough corners, using fine sandpaper.

Apply wood glue with a craft stick or dowel, spreading a thin, even layer over all surfaces that will be joined.

Slide glued surfaces back and forth against each other to create even contact and a firm bond.

Clamp the pieces together to hold them securely while reinforcing joints. Check for squareness by measuring diagonals. If pieces are square, diagonals will have the same measurement. If diagonals differ, adjust the pieces until the diagonals are equal.

Reinforce joints by drilling pilot holes through the joint and driving screws or finish nails into the holes. For screws, counterbore the pilot holes so the screw heads can be driven below the surface. For nails, countersink the nail heads with a nail set (page 35).

Fill counterbored holes with glued hardwood plugs, and countersunk nail holes with wood putty. After glue or putty dries, sand the surface smooth, then apply finish.

How to Make a Miter Joint

1 Mark moldings to the desired length, then set the blade on a miter saw to a 45° angle.

2 Hold or clamp the molding securely in the miter saw, then cut it to size. Apply a thin, even layer of wood glue to the mitered edges of the moldings.

3 Position the moldings on the workpiece with mitered ends tightly together. Drill pilot holes through the molding and into the workpiece, and attach the molding with finish nails.

How to Make Butt Joints

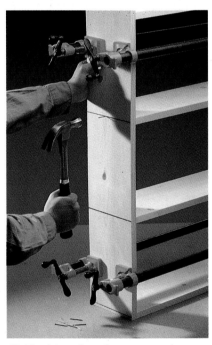

1 Outline the location of the joints on the workpiece, using a framing square as a guide. If desired, attach cleats (page 30) along the bottom edge of each joint to provide reinforcement.

2 Apply wood glue to the surfaces to be joined, using a craft stick or dowel to spread the glue evenly.

3 Position the pieces together, then reinforce each joint by drilling pilot holes and driving finish nails or screws through the joint. (Drawing a reference line on the workpiece can help you align the nails correctly.)

How to Make Dado Joints

1 Hold the pieces together and mark location of dado groove. Install a straight bit in a router, and set the bit to equal the depth of the planned dado. Dado depth generally is half as deep as the thickness of the wood; for 3/4"-thick wood, for example, dadoes should be 3/8" deep.

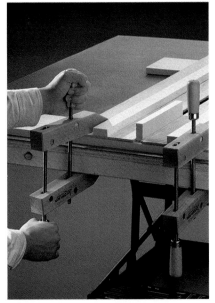

2 Clamp a straightedge guide (page 23) on each side of the planned dado, so the edges of the guides are against the marked lines. Set a piece of scrap wood the same thickness as the workpiece between the guides to check the spacing.

3 Cut the dado by making two passes with the router. Make the first pass with the base of the router held tightly against one straightedge cleat, then make the second pass in the opposite direction with the router base held against the other cleat.

4 Apply wood glue to the surfaces being joined, then clamp the pieces together. Reinforce each joint by drilling pilot holes and driving screws or finish nails spaced 3" to 4" apart. For screws, counterbore the pilot holes with a larger drill bit.

Circular saw dadoes: Cut along the marked outline, using a straightedge guide (page 23) and circular saw with blade set to equal the depth of the dado. Then make several parallel cuts inside the edge cuts, and clean out waste wood with a sharp chisel.

How to Make Rabbet Joints

Rabbet joints: Use a rabbet bit to rout edge grooves. Use a bit that is the same size as the thickness of the workpiece, and set the depth of cut to equal one-half the thickness. For example, for 3/4" workpieces, use a 3/4" rabbet bit set to 3/8" depth.

How to Make Blind Dowel Edge Joints Using a Dowel Jig

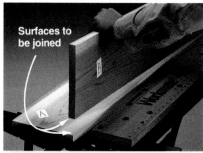

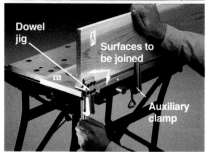

1 Align pieces as they will look when the joint is finished, and mark them A and B (top). Reverse the position of the pieces as shown (bottom) so surfaces being joined are facing you. Clamp the pieces together so the ends are aligned, using a dowel jig and auxiliary clamp.

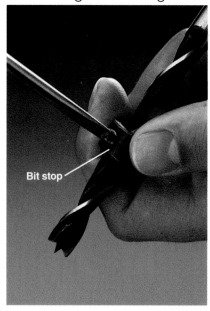

2 Mount a brad-point bit in a drill. Use a 3/8" bit if you will be doweling 3/4"-thick lumber. **TIP:** Attach a bit stop to the drill bit to ensure that you drill holes to the proper depth.

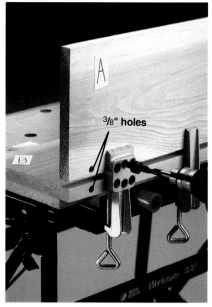

3 Drill dowel holes in both pieces through the jig opening that matches your bit size. For 3/4"-thick wood, holes in piece A should be 1/2" deep, and holes in B should be 1 1/4" deep. Reposition the jig and drill additional holes, spaced 3" to 4" apart. Leave auxiliary clamp in place when moving jig.

4 Test-fit the pieces by inserting fluted 1 1/2" dowels in piece A, then tapping piece B in place with a wood mallet. If pieces do not fit tightly, deepen the dowel holes in piece B.

5 Separate pieces and remove dowels, then apply glue to the dowels and insert them into holes in piece B. Also apply glue to the flat surfaces being joined. **NOTE:** When joining melamine-covered particleboard, apply glue to dowels only, not to the flat surfaces.

6 Assemble the pieces, tapping them with a wood mallet until the joint is snug. Completely wipe away any excess glue, using a damp cloth.

How to Make Blind Dowel Face Joints Using Dowel Centers

1 Mark the face of the workpiece to show location of joint. Make edge holes for dowels with a dowel jig (page opposite), then insert a dowel center in each hole.

2 Stand the pieces on edge on a flat surface, then force the pieces together so the sharp points on the dowel centers leave reference marks in the wood.

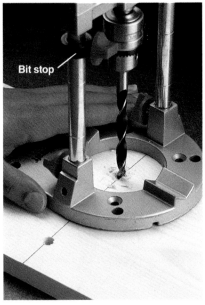

3 Drill holes at marked points, using a brad-point bit. For 3/4"-thick wood, holes should be 1/2" deep. Use a right-angle drill guide with bit stop to ensure straight, uniform holes. Assemble the workpiece with dowels (steps 4 to 6, page opposite).

How to Make Through-dowel Joints

1 Clamp and glue pieces together, and make a reference line to help you align the dowel holes. Then use a brad-point bit with a bit stop set to 1³/4" depth to drill dowel holes through one piece and into the adjoining piece. Space the holes 3" to 4" apart.

2 Apply wood glue to fluted 1¹/2" dowels, then insert the dowels into the holes. Drive the dowels to the bottoms of the holes, using a nail set.

3 Fill dowel holes with hardwood plugs coated with wood glue (page 31). Let the glue dry, then sand the plugged surface smooth.

How to Make Biscuit Joints

1 After cutting all pieces to size, identify and mark the orientation of each piece to make laying out biscuit positions easier, and to avoid confusion at glue-up time.

2 Place two pieces together and mark final assembly positions. Lay out biscuit positions 4"-6" apart and mark their centerlines on both workpieces. For perpendicular joints, clamp a straightedge in place to help hold the vertical piece for accurate marking.

3 Align the biscuit joiner (following manufacturer's directions) to a mark on workpiece. Clamp the piece securely, then hold the biscuit joiner firmly, and smoothly plunge the blade into the workpiece. Cut the other slots in the workpiece.

4 Follow the same directions to cut slots in the remaining workpieces. For perpendicular joints, after step 2, lay down the vertical piece so it aligns with the final assembly position. Cut the slots in the vertical piece, then use its end as a guide for cutting the slots in the face of the other workpiece.

5 After cutting all the slots, dry clamp the project together to make certain you have all the clamps, pads, and biscuits you need. Biscuits begin to swell as soon as glue is applied so having everything ready will allow you to work quickly.

6 Disassemble the project, then apply glue to the sides of the biscuit slots in mating pieces. Do not apply glue to the biscuits. After the slots, apply glue to the rest of the joining surfaces. Insert biscuits into slots, quickly clamp the project together, and allow glue to dry.

For mitered joints, attach the biscuit joiner's miter attachment to set the blade at the correct angle, usually 45°. This enables you to cut slots perpendicular to the miter edges. Glue and clamp in the same manner as with other biscuit joints.

1/4" glass

Melamine-covered particleboard

3/4" pine

3/4" finish-grade plywood

3/4" hardwood

3/4" finish-grade plywood edged with 1 × 2 hardwood

Double-layer plywood edged with hardwood molding

Shelves shown in order of strength

Adding Shelves

When making shelves for your built-in projects, choose shelving materials appropriate for the loads they must support. Thin glass shelves or particleboard can easily support light loads, like decorative glassware, but only the sturdiest shelves can hold a large television set or heavy reference books without bending or breaking.

The strength of a shelf also depends on its span—the distance between vertical risers. In general, shelves should be no more than 36" long.

Some shelves in built-ins are permanent features, joined to the body of the built-in using basic joinery methods (pages 30 to 35). Other shelves are adjustable, mounted with metal brackets or pin-style shelf supports. Adjustable shelves give more versatile storage, but permanent shelves are stronger. Permanent shelves also add structural reinforcement that improves the overall sturdiness of a built-in. Many built-ins include both permanent shelves for structural strength, and adjustable shelves for versatility.

Building your own shelves from finish-grade plywood edged with hardwood strips or moldings is a good choice for most built-in projects. Edged plywood shelves are strong, attractive, and much less expensive than solid hardwood shelves.

Attach hardwood edging or moldings to the front face of plywood shelves, using wood glue and finish nails. Position the edging so the top is slightly above the plywood surface, then drill pilot holes and drive finish nails. Use a nail set to countersink the nail heads. Sand the edging so it is smooth with the plywood surface before you finish the shelf. For greater strength, edge plywood shelves with 1 × 2 or 1 × 3 hardwood boards (photo, left).

How to Install Pin-style Supports for Adjustable Shelves

Drill-stop

1 Mount a drill and 1/4" bit in a right-angle drill guide, with drill-stop set for 3/8" depth. Align a pegboard scrap along the inside face of each riser, exactly flush with the end, to use as a template. Drill two rows of parallel holes in each riser, about 1 1/2" from the edges of riser, using the pegboard holes as a guide.

2 When built-in is completed, build shelves that are 1/8" shorter than the distance between risers. To mount each shelf, insert a pair of 1/4" pin-style shelf supports in each riser.

How to Install Metal Standards for Adjustable Shelves

1 Mark two parallel dado grooves on the inside face of each riser, using a marking gauge. Grooves should be at least 1" from the edges.

2 Cut dadoes to depth and thickness of metal standards, using a router (page 23). Test-fit standards to make sure they fit, then remove them.

3 After finishing the built-in, cut metal standards to fit into dadoes, and attach using nails or screws provided by manufacturer. Make sure slots in standards are aligned properly so shelves will be level.

4 Build shelves 1/8" shorter than the distance between risers, then insert shelf clips into the slots on the metal standards, and install shelves.

Adding Doors

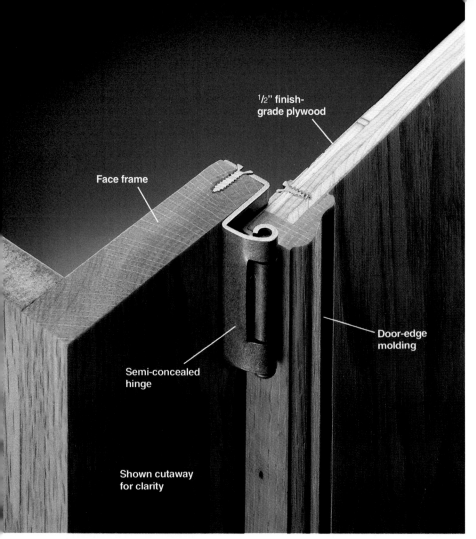

Face frame

1/2" finish-grade plywood

Semi-concealed hinge

Door-edge molding

Shown cutaway for clarity

Easy-to-build overlay doors, made with 1/2" finish-grade plywood panels framed with door-edge moldings, are designed to overhang the face frame by about 3/8" on each side. Semi-concealed overlay hinges, which require no mortising, are attached to the back of the door and to the edge of the face frame. This door style also can be adapted to make folding doors (page 115).

Cabinet doors are easy to make using 1/2" finish-grade plywood, and door-edge moldings. When hung with semi-concealed overlay hinges, do-it-yourself panel-style doors require no complicated routing or mortising techniques. You can build them to any size needed, and finish them to match your tastes.

Another easy option is to buy ready-made cabinet doors from a cabinet manufacturer or cabinet refacing company, and hang them yourself using semi-concealed hinges. You also can have a professional cabinetmaker design and build custom cabinet doors to your specifications—a good choice if you want wood-framed doors with glass panels.

Other do-it-yourself door options include sliding doors, solid-glass doors, and frameless doors (page opposite).

Door-catch hardware is recommended if your doors do not use self-closing hinges, or if you want to lock them. Common types of hardware include: utility hasp (A), roller catch (B), keyed lock (C), brass door bolt (D), and magnetic push latch (E) commonly used for solid glass doors.

Door Options

Ready-made cabinet doors are available in stock sizes from cabinet manufacturers and cabinet refacing companies. Or, you can have doors custom-built by a professional cabinetmaker. Install these doors with semi-concealed overlay hinges (steps 4 to 8, pages 42 to 43).

Sliding doors are a good choice if limited space makes it impractical to install swinging doors. Build a pair of sliding doors from 1/4" finish-grade plywood, cut so they are 1/2" shorter than the opening and will overlap by about 2" in the center. Attach door-track moldings to the top, bottom, and sides of the door opening. Install the doors by sliding them up into the top track, then lowering them into the bottom track.

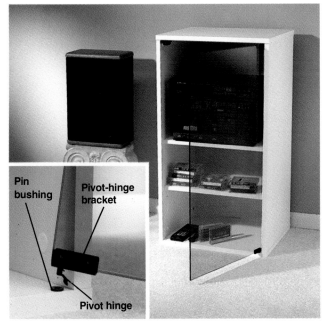

Pin bushing
Pivot-hinge bracket
Pivot hinge

Glass doors give a contemporary look to built-in projects. Use 1/4" tempered glass with smoothed edges, not ordinary window glass, for doors. To install a glass door, drill holes in the top and bottom of the door opening, and insert pivot-hinge bushings. Mount the door using pivot-hinge brackets attached to the glass with setscrews (inset).

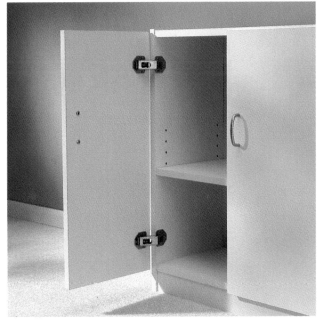

Frameless doors are common on contemporary-style built-ins constructed without face frames—especially those made with melamine-covered particleboard. Frameless doors are mounted with concealed hinges attached to the inside surface of the built-in.

How to Build & Install an Overlay Door

1 Measure the width and height of the door opening, and cut one or two door panels from 1/2" finish-grade plywood. (If opening is wider than 24", two doors are necessary.) **For two doors:** each door panel should equal the measured height of the opening; width of each panel will be one-half the total width of the opening, minus 1/2". (For example, if opening is 14" high and 36" wide, each door panel should be 14" high and 17 1/2" wide.) **For one door:** door panel should equal the width and height of the door opening.

2 For each door, measure and cut door-edge molding to frame the door panel, mitering the ends at a 45° angle.

3 Attach door-edge molding to door panel by drilling pilot holes and driving 1 1/2" finish nails through the side of the molding and into the door panels. Finish the door to match the built-in.

4 Mount two semi-concealed overlay hinges to the back of the door, 2" from the top and bottom. **NOTE:** Use three hinges, evenly spaced, if the door is taller than 30".

5 Use masking tape to mark a reference line on the top face frame rail, 1/2" above the door opening.

6 Position the door over the opening, aligning the top edge with the tape reference line. Mark one hinge location on the face frame with masking tape.

7 Open the hinges, and position the door against the edge of the face frame so the hinge is aligned with the tape marking the hinge locations. Drill pilot holes, and anchor the hinges to the face frame with the mounting screws. Remove the masking tape.

8 Attach door handles or knobs, and any door catch hardware you desire, following manufacturer's directions.

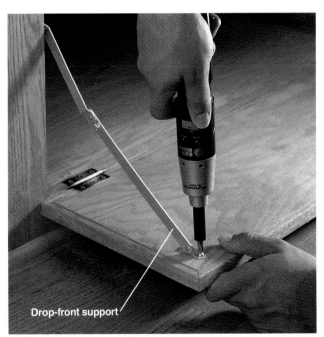

Drop-front support

Drop-down door variation: Build an overlay door as directed above, but attach the semi-concealed hinges to the bottom face frame rail. Attach drop-front supports on both sides of the door opening to support the door, and install door-catch hardware to keep it from falling open.

Adding Drawers

Most built-ins can be adapted to include drawers. In addition to providing useful storage, drawers and decorative hardware make a built-in more attractive.

In its simplest form, a drawer is nothing more than a wooden box that slides back and forth on a permanent shelf. By adding drawer slide hardware, a hardwood drawer face, and ornamental knobs or pulls, you can make drawers look more professional.

Ready-made hardwood drawer faces are sold by companies specializing in cabinet refacing products. Or, you can make your own drawer faces by cutting hardwood boards and using a router to give them decorative edges.

Drawers can be constructed in many different styles, but the drawer shown on the following pages is simple to build and will work for any of the built-in projects in this book. This design is called an "overlay" drawer because it features a hardwood drawer face that overhangs the cabinet face frame by 1/2".

Drawer pulls and knobs help define the overall style of your project. If your built-in also includes cabinet doors with handles or pulls, buy all door and drawer hardware at the same time to ensure a good match. For drawers wider than 24", install two knobs or pulls.

Tips for Building Drawers

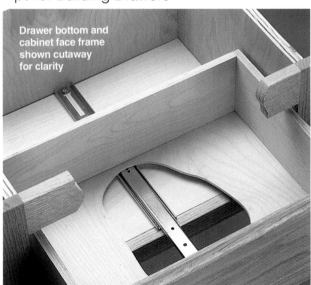

Choose center-mounted drawer slides with steel ball-bearing rollers. Center-mounted slides, like the Accuride® slide shown above, are easier to install than side-mounted slides, and those with steel ball-bearings are much more durable than those with plastic rollers. Specify the depth of your drawers when buying drawer slides.

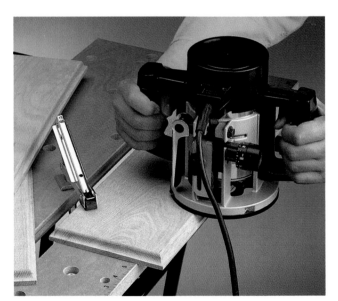

Make your own drawer faces by cutting hardwood boards to the proper size, then routing ornamental edges on them with a decorative router bit, like an ogee bit. To ensure smooth edges, make the cuts with several passes of the router; begin with the bit set to a shallow depth, then gradually extend the bit until you achieve the desired appearance.

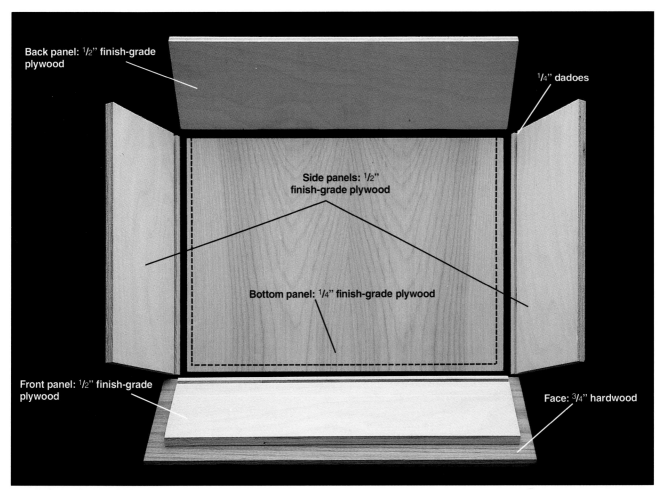

Back panel: 1/2" finish-grade plywood

Side panels: 1/2" finish-grade plywood

1/4" dadoes

Bottom panel: 1/4" finish-grade plywood

Front panel: 1/2" finish-grade plywood

Face: 3/4" hardwood

Anatomy of an overlay drawer: The basic drawer box is made using 1/2" plywood for the front, back, and side panels, with a 1/4" plywood bottom panel. The bottom panel fits into 1/4" dadoes cut near the bottom of the front and side panels, and is nailed to the bottom edge of the back panel. The hardwood drawer face is screwed to the drawer front from the inside, and is sized so it overhangs the face frame by 1/2" on all sides. **NOTE:** This drawer is designed to be mounted with a center-mounted drawer slide attached to the bottom of the drawer (page opposite). If you use different hardware, like side-mounted drawer slides, you will need to alter this design according to slide manufacturer's directions.

How to Measure for an Overlay Drawer

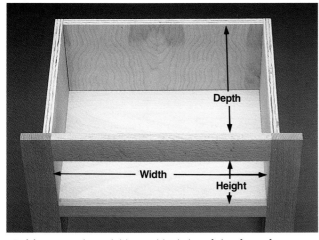

Depth

Width

Height

Part		Measurement
Sides	length	Depth of opening, minus 3"
	height	Height of opening, minus 1/2"
Front	length	Width of opening, minus 1 1/2"
	height	Height of opening, minus 1/2"
Back	length	Width of opening, minus 1 1/2"
	height	Height of opening, minus 1"
Bottom	width	Width of opening, minus 1"
	depth	Depth of opening, minus 2 3/4"
Face	length	Width of opening, plus 1"
	height	Height of opening, plus 1"

1 Measure the width and height of the face frame opening, and the depth of the cabinet from face frame to back panel.

2 Calculate the sizes for each drawer part using the table above. Cut and assemble the drawer by following the directions on the following pages.

How to Build & Install an Overlay Drawer

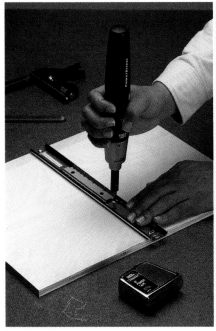
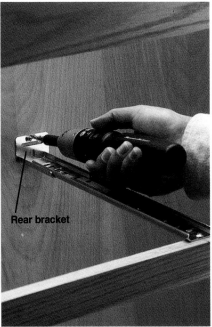
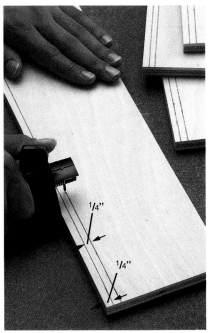

1 Install the track for the center-mounted drawer slide, as directed by the manufacturer. If the slide track will rest on a permanent shelf (left), it is easiest to install it on the shelf before assembling the built-in. If the slide will be supported by the face frame and the back panel (right), mount the slide using the rear bracket included with the drawer slide kit.

2 Measure the drawer opening, then cut all drawer pieces to size (page 45). Outline ¼"-wide dado grooves on the inside faces of the side and front panels, ¼" from the bottom edges, using a marking gauge as a guide.

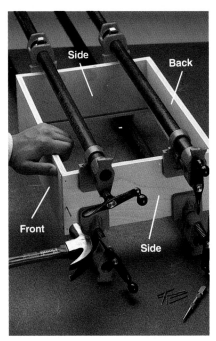

3 Cut ¼" deep dadoes along the marked outlines, using a router and ¼" straight bit. Use a router edge guide (page 23) to ensure straight cuts.

4 Clamp and glue the front, back, and side panels together, so front and back panels are between the side panels, and the top edges of panels are aligned. Reinforce each corner with 2" finish nails driven through the joints.

5 Let glue dry, then remove the clamps. From the back of the drawer box, slide the drawer bottom panel fully into the dado grooves. Do not apply glue to the dadoes or the bottom panel.

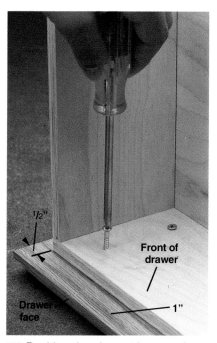

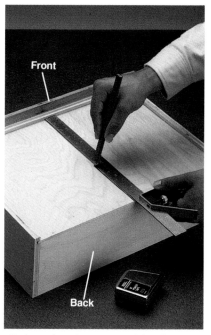

6 Attach the rear edge of the bottom panel to the back panel with wire nails spaced every 4".

7 Position the drawer box against the back side of the drawer face, so the face overhangs by 1/2" on the sides and bottom, and 1" on the top. Attach the face with 1" screws driven into the drawer face from inside the drawer box.

8 Lay the drawer upside down, then measure and mark a center line along the bottom panel from front to back.

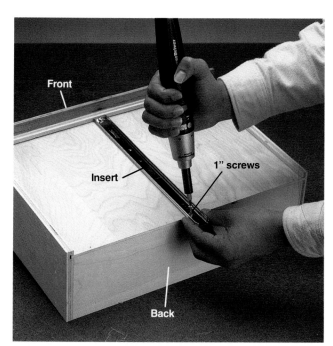

9 Center the drawer slide insert over the marked center line, and attach it with a 1" screw driven through the drawer bottom and into the back panel, and another screw driven diagonally into the drawer front panel.

10 Install the drawer by lining up the insert with the track, then gently pushing the drawer in until the insert and track lock together. Attach drawer pulls or knobs, if desired.

Halogen lights

Wire tracks

Add low-voltage light fixtures to highlight favorite items and add visual interest to any built-in project. Low-voltage halogen lights, like those shown above, use very little electricity, and can be left on permanently. Wires for low-voltage lights run through small dado grooves cut into the shelves and risers, and are covered with plastic wire tracks inserted in the dadoes. Leave several inches of open space between lights and stored items to prevent heat from building up.

Adding Electrical Accessories

Transformer

Adding electrical accessories to your built-in projects makes them more attractive and useful. An ordinary bookcase becomes an elegant display case when you add built-in lighting fixtures. Installing a convenient electrical outlet strip in the back of an entertainment center lets you connect electronic equipment without using cumbersome, dangerous extension cords.

When adding lights or other electrical accessories to a built-in, try to position the wires so they are hidden from view. Inexpensive plastic wire organizers and wire tracks attached inside a built-in help hide electrical cords and prevent them from tangling.

A 12-volt transformer converts 120-volt current from an ordinary wall receptacle to provide power for low-voltage lights, like those shown above.

Helpful Electrical Accessories

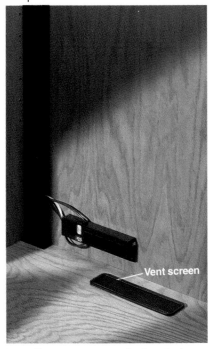

Vent screen

Install vent screens in the shelves or walls of your built-in to help dissipate heat if your built-in will contain electronic equipment, like a television, computer, stereo, or microwave oven.

An outlet strip attached inside a built-in provides a convenient place to plug in a television, stereo, computer, or light fixtures. Some models have a remote on-off switch to control up to four receptacles, and may include a telephone jack or cable TV outlet. Outlet strips with power-surge protection are essential for use with a computer.

A wire organizer tacked inside a built-in hides and organizes electrical cords and cables. Wire organizers are made of plastic, and can be cut to any length you need.

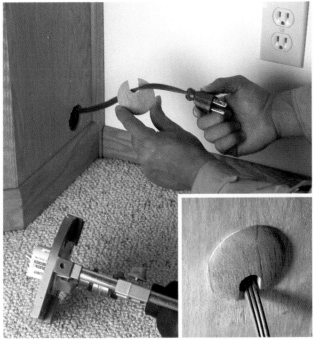

Grommet plates help hide the holes that have been drilled to run cords and cables through the sides of a built-in. Drill the holes with a hole saw or forstner bit to reduce splintering. Grommets are available in a variety of materials, including hardwood, which can be finished to match most wood surfaces (inset).

Built-In Projects

See page 9 for more ideas for using recessed wall shelves

Building Recessed Wall Shelves

Installing recessed shelving is one of the easiest built-in projects. This project consists of a shallow wooden box that is inserted in a wall cutout and framed with hardwood. Recessed shelves can be installed in almost any interior wall, except in areas where electrical wires or plumbing pipes are located.

The project as shown is 30" wide—the width of two stud cavities in a standard wall built with studs spaced 16" on-center. To duplicate these shelves, you will need to cut away one wall stud

and install a sill and header. Never cut away more than one stud when building recessed shelving. You may, however, build a narrower cabinet by building the shelves into a single stud cavity between adjacent studs.

Everything You Need:

Tools: pencil, level, jig saw, reciprocating saw, power screwdriver, drill, right-angle drill guide, pegboard scraps, pipe clamps, hammer, tape measure, utility knife.

Materials: wood glue, 1 1/2" finish nails, wood screws (1 1/2", 2 1/2"), 1" wire nails, pin-style shelf supports, wood shims.

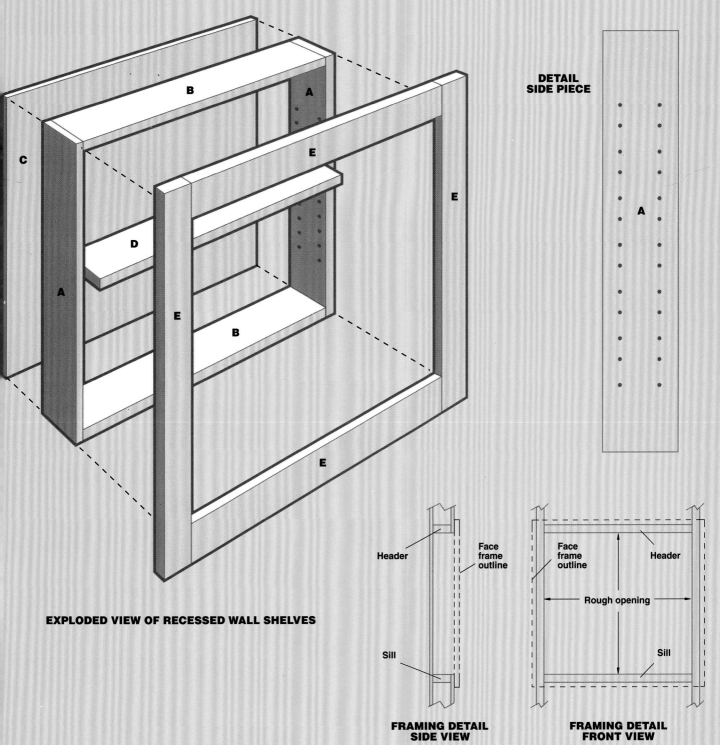

DETAIL
SIDE PIECE

A

EXPLODED VIEW OF RECESSED WALL SHELVES

Header

Face
frame
outline

Sill

**FRAMING DETAIL
SIDE VIEW**

Face
frame
outline

Header

Rough opening

Sill

**FRAMING DETAIL
FRONT VIEW**

Parts List: Recessed Wall Shelves

Project as Shown					Your Project	
Key	**Piece**	**Material**	**Pieces**	**Size**	**Pieces**	**Size**
A	Sides	1 × 4 oak	2	30"		
B	Top & bottom	1 × 4 oak	2	$28^{3}/_{4}$"		
C	Back panel	$^{1}/_{4}$" oak plywood	1	$30 \times 29^{1}/_{2}$"		
D	Shelves	1 × 4 oak	3	$28^{5}/_{8}$"		
E	Face frame	1 × 4 oak	11 linear ft.			
F	Header and sill plates	2 × 4	2	$30^{1}/_{2}$"		

53

How to Build Recessed Shelving

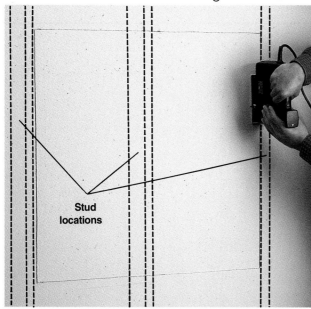

1 Locate wall studs in area where shelves will be installed. Mark the cutout on the wall, using a level as a guide. Sides of cutout should follow edges of wall studs, and height of cutout should allow for the thickness of a header and sill plate. Make the cutout with a jigsaw. **CAUTION:** Check for plumbing and electrical cables before cutting into any wall.

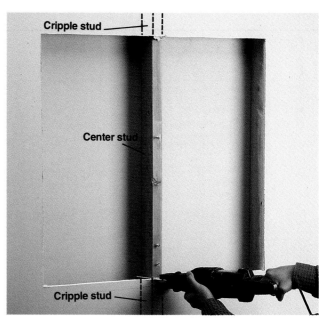

2 Cut away the center stud at the top and bottom edge of the opening, using a reciprocating saw. Use a flat pry bar to remove the cut portion of stud. (You may need to patch the opposite wall surface if it is screwed or nailed to the stud you remove.)

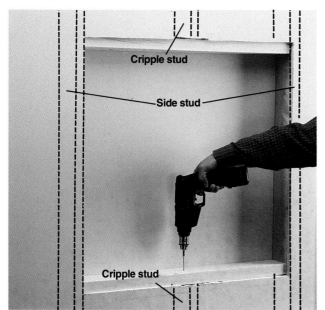

3 Measure between side studs at top and bottom edges of opening, and cut header and sill plates to fit. Attach header and sill to cripple studs and side studs with 3" screws. Remeasure the height of the opening between the installed header and sill plates. Cut side pieces 1³/4" shorter than the measured height of the opening. Cut 1 × 4 top and bottom pieces ¹/4" shorter than the measured width to allow for small adjustments during installation.

4 Drill two rows of holes on the inside face of each side piece to hold pin-style shelf supports (page 39). Use a right-angle drill guide, and use a scrap piece of pegboard as a template to ensure that the holes on facing pieces will be lined up properly.

5 Glue and clamp the side pieces around the top and bottom pieces to form butt joints (page 32). Drill counterbored pilot holes into the joints, and reinforce them with 1½" wood screws. You could also use biscuit joints (page 36) for a stronger connection.

6 Measure and cut ¼" plywood back panel to fit flush with the outside edges of the frame. Attach with 1" wire nails driven every 4" or 5". To allow for natural expansion and contraction, do not glue the back panel.

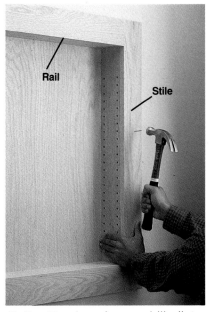

7 Position box in opening and shim until it is level and plumb and front edges are flush with wall surface. Drill pilot holes, and anchor cabinet to side studs, header and sill, using ½" finish nails driven every 4" to 5" and through shim locations. Trim shims with a utility knife.

8 Measure the inside height and width of cabinet box, then cut 1 × 3 horizontal face frame rails equal to width, and 1 × 3 vertical stiles 5" longer than height. Glue and clamp rails between stiles to form butt joints, and reinforce joints by drilling pilot holes and driving 3" finish nails through stiles and into rails.

9 Position face frame, drill pilot holes, and attach with 1½" finish nails driven into the top, bottom, and side panels and into the framing members. Countersink nails, fill nail holes, sand, and finish the project. Build and install adjustable shelves (page 39) ⅛" shorter than distance between side panels.

Building a Kneewall Cabinet

A kneewall is a short wall that meets the slope of the roofline in an upstairs room. By cutting a hole in a kneewall and installing a recessed cabinet, you can turn the wasted space behind it into a useful storage area.

Because the body (carcass) of a kneewall cabinet is not visible, it can be built using ordinary plywood and simple butt joints. The face frame and drawer faces, however, should be built with hardwood, and finished carefully.

The project shown here fits in a space that is 30" wide—the standard width of two adjacent stud cavities with a center stud removed. Before beginning work, check the spacing of studs and the location of electrical or plumbing lines behind your kneewall. Your kneewall may have a removable access panel, which makes it easy to check behind the wall.

You can make the cabinet wider or narrower to fit your wall stud spacing, but regardless of size, be sure to leave a few inches of space between the back of the cabinet and the rafters.

Everything You Need:

Tools: level, circular saw or jigsaw, flat pry bar, reciprocating saw, drill, tape measure, bar clamps, hammer, nail set.

Materials: power-driver screws (1", 2", 3"), finish nails (1 1/2", 2", 3"), wood glue, finishing materials, drawer hardware.

See page 8 for more kneewall cabinet ideas

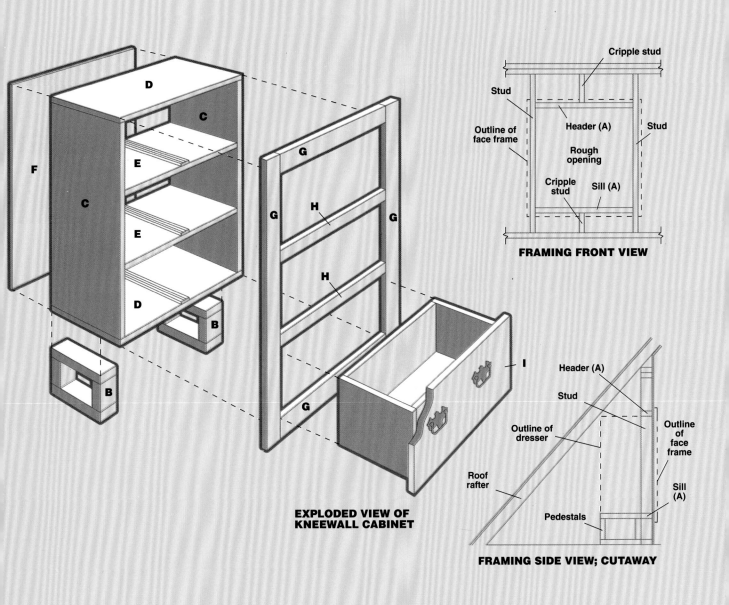

FRAMING FRONT VIEW

Cripple stud

Stud

Header (A)

Stud

Outline of face frame

Rough opening

Cripple stud

Sill (A)

EXPLODED VIEW OF KNEEWALL CABINET

FRAMING SIDE VIEW; CUTAWAY

Header (A)

Stud

Outline of dresser

Outline of face frame

Sill (A)

Roof rafter

Pedestals

Parts List: Kneewall Cabinet

		Project as Shown			Your Project	
Key	**Part**	**Material**	**Pieces**	**Size**	**Pieces**	**Size**
A	Header and sill	2 × 4s	6 linear ft.			
B	Pedestals	2 × 4s	2	14" × 15"		
C	Sides	3/4" plywood	2	28 1/2" × 19"		
D	Top and bottom	3/4" plywood	2	30" × 19"		
E	Shelves	3/4" plywood	2	28 1/2" × 19"		
F	Back panel	1/4" plywood	1	30" × 30"		
G	Face frame	1 × 4 oak	11 linear ft.			
H	Shelf rails	1 × 2 oak	5 linear ft.			
I	Drawers	see pages 44 to 47				

Kneewall Cabinet Project Details

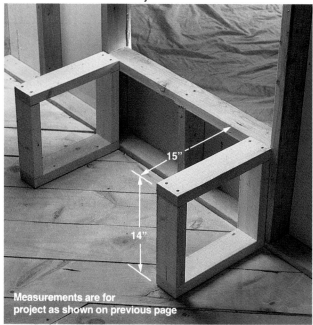

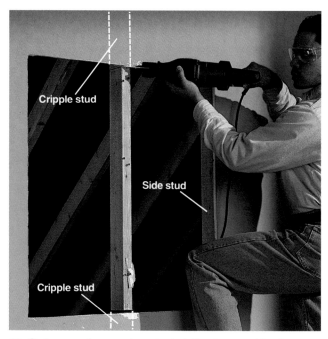

Measurements are for project as shown on previous page

15"

14"

Measurements are for project as shown on previous page

1 × 2 shelf rails

1 × 4 rails

8¹/₂" × 28¹/₂" opening

1 × 4 stiles

Pedestals installed behind the kneewall create a sturdy base for the cabinet. Built from 2 × 4s, the pedestals raise the cabinet so it fits above the baseboard. Raising the cabinet also makes drawers more accessible.

Face frame is 1 × 4 hardwood, which will cover the rough edges of the wall opening. The shelf rails are made from 1 × 2 hardwood to maximize the size of the drawer openings.

How to Build a Kneewall Cabinet

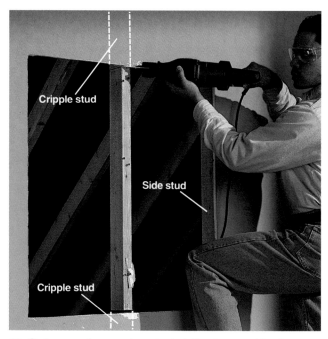

Cripple stud

Side stud

Cripple stud

1 Locate wall studs in area where cabinet will be installed. Mark the cutout on the wall, using a level as a guide. Bottom of cutout should be at least 3" above baseboard, and sides of cutout should follow edges of wall studs. Height of cutout should be 3¹/₄" taller than overall height of cabinet, to allow space for a header and sill. **CAUTION:** Check for wiring, pipes, and duct work before cutting into any wall.

2 Cut away the center stud at the top and bottom of the opening, using a reciprocating saw. Remove the stud. Remaining portions of cut studs are called "cripple" studs.

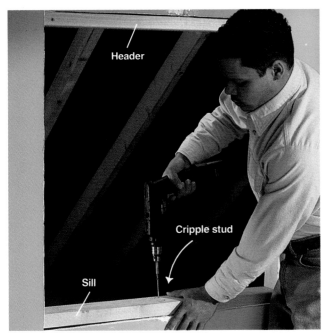

3 Measure and cut a 2 × 4 header and sill to fit snugly between side studs. Position in opening, check for level, and shim if necessary. Attach the header and sill to the cripple studs and side studs, using 3" screws.

4 Measure the distance from the floor behind the opening to the top of the sill, and build two 2 × 4 pedestals to this height (see Project Details, page 58). Join pedestal pieces together with glue and 3" screws.

5 Set the pedestals on the floor inside the wall opening, even with the sides of the framed opening. Check to make sure pedestals are level, and shim between the pedestals and the floor if necessary. Attach pedestals to the floor, using 3" screws.

6 Measure width and height of the rough opening between framing members. Cut side panels 2" shorter than the height of rough opening. Cut top and bottom panels 1/2" shorter than the width of rough opening. Cut shelves 1 1/2" shorter than the width of the opening.

(continued next page)

7 Attach drawer slide tracks to the center of the bottom panel and the shelves (pages 44 to 46), following manufacturer's directions.

8 Clamp and glue the shelves to the side panels to form butt joints (pages 31 to 32). Reinforce the joints with 2" screws driven through the side panels and into the edges of shelves.

9 Clamp and glue the top and bottom panels to the side panels, then reinforce the joints with 2" screws.

10 Measure and cut 1/4" plywood panel to cover the back of the cabinet. Attach with 1" screws or wire nails driven through the back and into the side, top, and bottom panels. To allow for expansion and contraction of wood, do not use wood glue on this joint.

11 Measure the width and height between the inside edges of the cabinet. Cut the rails to the width. Cut the stiles to the height plus 7". Clamp and glue rails between stiles, and reinforce joints by toenailing 3" finish nails through the rails and into the stiles. Or you can use biscuit joints to connect the rails and stiles.

12 Apply glue to edges of cabinet, then position face frame over cabinet so inside edges of the face frame are flush with the top, bottom, and side panels. Attach the face frame by drilling pilot holes and driving 1¹/₂" finish nails into the cabinet every 8". Use a nail set to countersink the nail heads.

13 Slide the cabinet into the opening so it rests on the pedestals and the face frame is against the wall surface.

14 Anchor the cabinet by drilling pilot holes and driving 3" finish nails through the face frame and into the wall framing members. Also, drive 3" finish nails through the bottom of the cabinet and into the sill.

15 Sand and finish the cabinet face frame, then build, finish, and install overlay drawers (pages 44 to 47).

See page 15 for more utility shelf ideas

Building Utility Shelves

You can build adjustable utility shelves in a single afternoon using 2 × 4s and plain 3/4" plywood. Perfect for use in a garage or basement, utility shelves can be modified by adding side panels and a face frame to create a finished look suitable for a family room or recreation area.

The quick-and-easy shelf project shown on the following pages creates two columns of shelves with a total width of 68". You can enlarge the project easily by adding more 2 × 4 risers and plywood shelves (do not increase the individual shelf widths to more than 36"). The sole plates for the utility shelves are installed perpendicular

to the wall to improve access to the space under the bottom shelves.

Everything You Need:

Tools: pencil, tape measure, level, framing square, power screwdriver, plumb bob, stud gun (concrete floors only), clamps, router with 3/4" straight bit, circular saw, stepladder.

Materials: wood glue, shims, power-driver screws (2½", 3"), finishing materials.

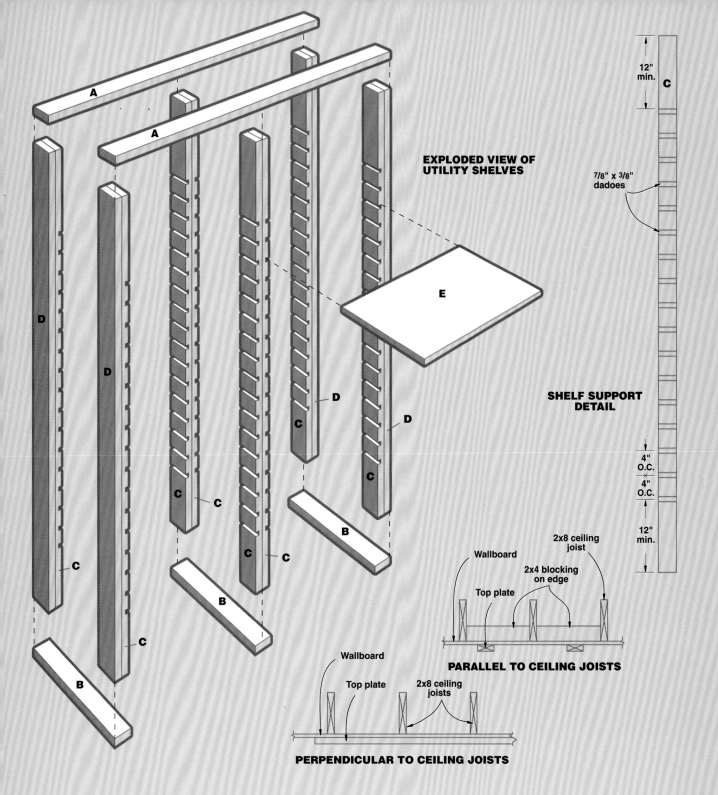

EXPLODED VIEW OF UTILITY SHELVES

SHELF SUPPORT DETAIL

12" min.

C

7/8" x 3/8" dadoes

4" O.C.

4" O.C.

12" min.

PARALLEL TO CEILING JOISTS

2x8 ceiling joist

2x4 blocking on edge

Top plate

Wallboard

PERPENDICULAR TO CEILING JOISTS

Wallboard

Top plate

2x8 ceiling joists

Parts List: Utility Shelves

		Project as Shown			Your Project	
Key	Part	Material	Pieces	Size	Pieces	Size
A	Top plates	2 × 4s	2	68"		
B	Sole plates	2 × 4s	3	24"		
C	Shelf risers	2 × 4s	8	93"		
D	End risers	2 × 4s	4	93"		
E	Shelves	3/4" plywood	12	30 3/4" × 24"		

How to Build Utility Shelves

1 Mark location of top plates on ceiling. One plate should be flush against wall, and the other should be parallel to first plate, with front edge 24" from the wall. Cut 2 × 4 top plates to full length of utility shelves, then attach to ceiling joists or blocking (page 29), using 3" screws.

2 Mark points directly beneath outside corners of the top plates to find outer sole plate locations, using a plumb bob as a guide (top). Mark sole plate locations by drawing lines perpendicular to the wall connecting each pair of points (bottom).

3 Cut outer 2 × 4 sole plates and position them perpendicular to the wall, just inside the outlines. Shim plates to level if needed, then attach to floor with a stud gun or 3" screws. Attach a center sole plate midway between the outer sole plates.

4 Prepare the shelf risers by cutting 7/8"-wide, 3/4"-deep dadoes with a router. Cut dadoes every 4" along the inside face of each 2 × 4 riser, with the top and bottom dadoes cut about 12" from the ends of the 2 × 4. **TIP:** Gang-cut the risers by laying them flat and clamping them together, then attaching a straightedge guide (page 23) to align the dado cuts. For each cut, make several passes with the router, gradually extending the bit depth until dadoes are 3/4" deep.

5 Trim the shelf risers to uniform length before unclamping them. Use a circular saw and a straightedge guide.

6 Build two center shelf supports by positioning pairs of shelf risers back-to-back and joining them with wood glue and 2¹/₂" screws.

7 Build four end shelf supports by positioning the back of a dadoed shelf riser against a 2 × 4 of the same length, then joining the 2 × 4 and the riser with glue and 2¹/₂" screws.

8 Position an end shelf support at each corner of the shelving unit, between top and sole plates. Attach the supports by driving 3" screws "toenail" style into the top plate and sole plates.

9 Position a center shelf support (both faces dadoed) at each end of the center sole plate, then anchor shelf supports to the sole plate using 3" screws driven "toenail" style. Use a framing square to align the center shelf supports perpendicular to the top plates, then anchor to top plates.

10 Measure distance between facing dado grooves, subtract ¹/₄", then cut plywood shelves to fit. Slide the shelves into the grooves.

See page 10 for more project ideas

Building Floor-to-Ceiling Shelves

Floor-to-ceiling shelves are sturdier and make better use of space than freestanding bookcases. When finished and trimmed to match the surrounding room, floor-to-ceiling shelves turn an ordinary room into an inviting den or library.

This project uses finish-grade oak plywood and a solid oak face frame to give this project the look of an expensive, solid oak shelf unit—but at a fraction of the cost. The plywood panels are supported and strengthened by an internal framework of 2 × 4 stud lumber.

When installing floor-to-ceiling shelves in a corner, as shown here, add 1/2" plywood spacers to the support studs that adjoin the wall. Spacers ensure that face frame stiles of equal width can be installed at both shelf ends (see diagram, page opposite).

Everything You Need:

Tools: tape measure, pencil, level, framing square, plumb bob, drill, hammer, circular saw, router, 3/4" straight bit.

Materials: shims, power-driver screws (13/4", 2", 3"), finish nails (11/2", 2"), metal shelf standards and clips, finishing materials, door and drawer hardware, 1/2" plywood scraps.

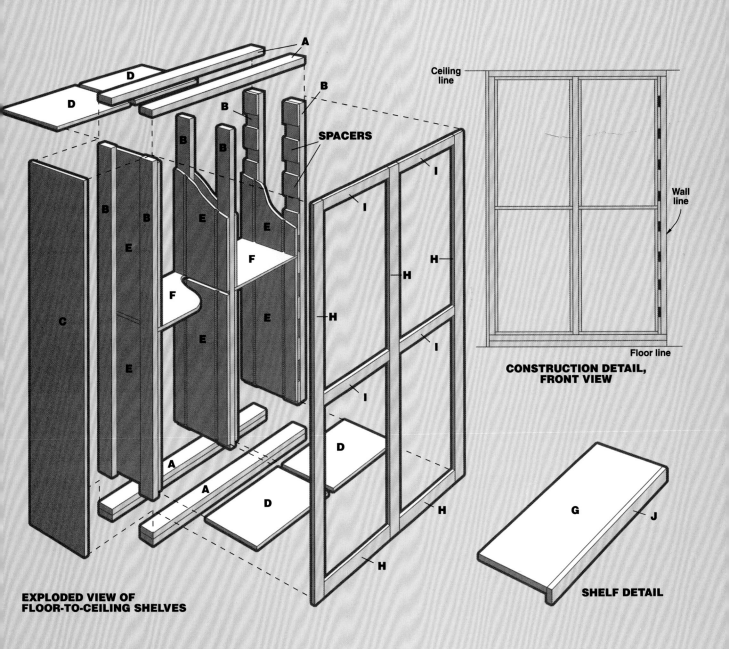

EXPLODED VIEW OF FLOOR-TO-CEILING SHELVES

SPACERS

Ceiling line

Wall line

Floor line

CONSTRUCTION DETAIL, FRONT VIEW

SHELF DETAIL

Parts List: Floor-to-Ceiling Shelves

	Project as Shown				Your Project	
Key	Part	Material	Pieces	Size	Pieces	Size
A	Top and sole plates	2 × 4s	6	59$\frac{1}{2}$"		
B	Support studs	2 × 4s	6	91$\frac{1}{2}$"		
C	End panel	$\frac{1}{2}$" oak plywood	1	95$\frac{3}{4}$" × 13"		
D	Top, bottom panels	$\frac{1}{2}$" oak plywood	4	27$\frac{1}{4}$" × 13"		
E	Risers	$\frac{1}{2}$" oak plywood	8	44$\frac{7}{8}$" × 13"		
F	Permanent shelves	$\frac{3}{4}$" oak plywood	2	27$\frac{1}{4}$" × 13"		
G	Adjustable shelves	$\frac{3}{4}$" oak plywood	8	26$\frac{1}{8}$" × 11$\frac{7}{8}$"		
H	Stiles and bottom rail	1 × 4 oak	28 linear ft.			
I	Top rail, middle rail	1 × 3 oak	10 linear ft.			
J	Shelf edging	1 × 2 oak	18 linear ft.			

How to Build Floor-to-Ceiling Shelves

1 Mark the location for two parallel 2 × 4 top plates on the ceiling, using a framing square as a guide. The front edge of the outer top plate should be 13" from back wall, and the other top plate should be flush against the wall. Mark location of ceiling joists; if necessary, install blocking between joists (page 29) to provide a surface for anchoring the top plates.

2 Measure and cut 2 × 4 top plates. Position each plate, check to make sure it is level, and shim if necessary. Attach plates to ceiling with 3" screws driven into the joists or blocking.

3 Cut 2 × 4 sole plates and screw them together to form two doubled sole plates. Use a plumb bob suspended from the outside corners of the top plates to align the sole plates, then shim to level, if needed; anchor the plates by driving 3" screws toenail-style into the floor.

4 Install 2 × 4 support studs between the ends of the top plates and sole plates. Attach support studs with 3" screws driven toenail-style into the top plates and sole plates.

5 Install center support studs midway between the end support studs. Attach to bottom plate first, using 3" screws driven toenail-style. Use a level to make sure that stud is plumb, then attach the studs to the top plate with 3" screws.

6 Where the shelves fit into a corner, use 2" screws to attach 1/2" plywood spacers on the inside faces of the support studs, spaced every 4". Make sure spacers do not extend past the front face of the studs.

7 Where the end of the project is exposed, measure and cut a 1/2" plywood end panel to floor-to-ceiling height. Attach the panel to the support studs so the front edges are flush, using 1 3/4" screws driven through the support studs and into the end panel.

8 Measure and cut 1/2" plywood top and bottom panels to fit between the support studs. Attach to the top and sole plates using 1 1/2" finish nails.

9 Measure and cut lower risers from 1/2" plywood, then cut dadoes for metal shelf standards (page 39).

10 Install lower risers on each side of the 2 × 4 support studs so the front edges are flush with the edges of the studs. Attach risers with 1 1/2" finish nails driven into the support studs. For riser that adjoins wall, drive nails at spacer locations.

11 Measure and cut permanent shelves from 3/4" plywood to fit between the support studs, just above the lower risers. Set shelves on risers and attach them with 1 1/2" finish nails driven down into the risers.

(continued next page)

12 Measure and cut upper risers to fit between the permanent shelves and the top panels. Cut dadoes for metal shelf standards, then attach the risers to the support studs with 1¹/2" finish nails.

13 Measure and cut 1 × 3 stiles to reach from floor to ceiling along the front edges of the exposed support studs. Drill pilot holes and attach the stiles to the support studs so they are flush with the risers, using glue and 1¹/2" finish nails driven at 8" intervals into the studs and risers.

14 Measure and cut 1 × 3 top rails to fit between the stiles. Drill pilot holes and attach the rails to the top plate and top panels, using glue and 1¹/2" finish nails.

15 Measure and cut 1 × 4 bottom rails to fit between the stiles. Drill pilot holes, and attach the rails to the sole plates and bottom panels, using glue and 1¹/2" finish nails. The top edge of the rails should be flush with the top surface of the plywood panels.

16 Fill nail holes, then sand and finish the wood surfaces.

17 Measure, cut, and install metal shelf standards into the dadoes (page 39), using nails or screws provided by the manufacturer.

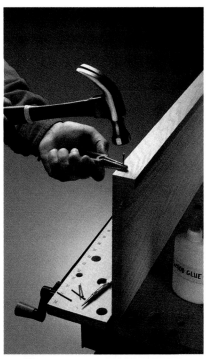

18 Measure and cut adjustable shelves 1/8" shorter than the distance between metal standards. Cut shelf edging, and attach with glue and 1 1/2" finish nails. Sand and finish the shelves.

19 Insert shelf clips into metal shelf standards and install the adjustable shelves at desired heights.

20 Cover gaps between the project and walls and floor with molding that has been finished to match the shelf unit.

See page 11 for more platform bench ideas

Building a Platform Bench

A platform bench combines convenient storage with a generous seating area. Because of its low profile and adaptability, a platform bench fits nicely into many locations: next to a built-in bookcase, in a window bay, or along a flat wall beneath a picture window. When used as a window seat, a platform bench is a perfect spot for relaxing on a sunny morning. Cushions and throw pillows soften the look and feel of the bench. And when aromatic cedar panels are added, the interior of the built-in becomes an ideal storage space for quilts and fine linens.

The platform bench shown here is 21" high, 24" deep, and 48" long. With careful cutting, the main panels of the project may be cut from a single 4 ft. × 8 ft. sheet of oak plywood. By raising or lowering the height of the side panels, you can adapt the design to any height you find comfortable, though you may need additional plywood.

If you build a platform bench more than 48" long, add a vertical face frame stile in the center of the opening for extra support.

Everything You Need:

Tools: tape measure, level, pencil, power screwdriver, drill, circular saw, wood chisel, hammer, nail set, clamps, dowel jig.

Materials: shims, finish nails (1", 2"), power-driver screws (1/2", 2", 21/2", 3"), fluted dowels, glue, aromatic cedar panels, semi-concealed hinges, door catches, finishing materials, wood plugs, corner brackets, door hardware.

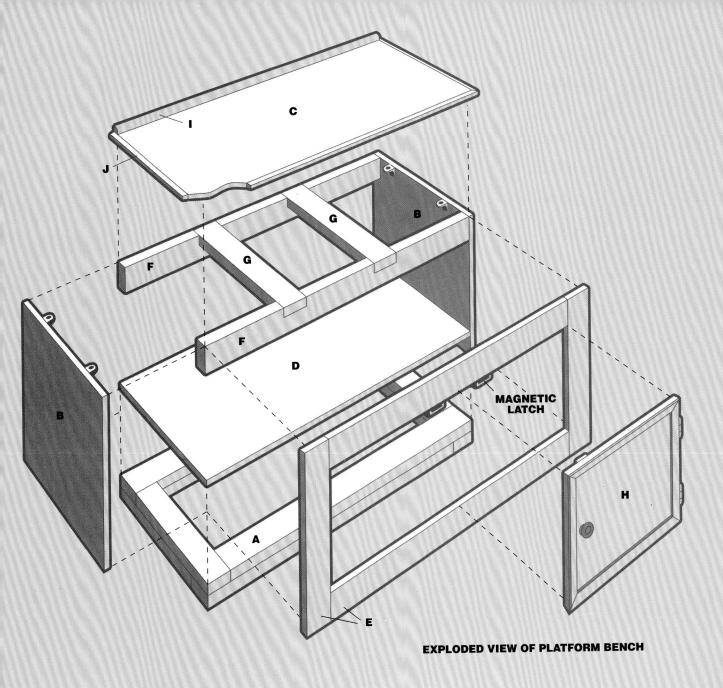

EXPLODED VIEW OF PLATFORM BENCH

MAGNETIC LATCH

Parts List: Platform Bench

Project as Shown					Your Project	
Key	Part	Material	Pieces	Size	Pieces	Size
A	Pedestals	2 × 4s	2	$46^1/2" \times 24"$		
B	Side panels	$3/4"$ oak plywood	2	$24" \times 21"$		
C	Top panel (seat)	$3/4"$ oak plywood	1	$48" \times 24^3/4"$		
D	Bottom panel	$3/4"$ oak plywood	1	$46^1/2" \times 24"$		
E	Face frame	1 × 4 oak	12 linear ft.			
F	Supports	2 × 4	2	$46^1/2"$		
G	Cross braces	2 × 4	2	24"		
H	Overlay doors		see pages 40 to 43			
I	Trim	Base shoe molding	12 linear ft.			
J	Top panel edging	Shelf-edge molding	7 linear ft.			

73

Platform Bench Project Details

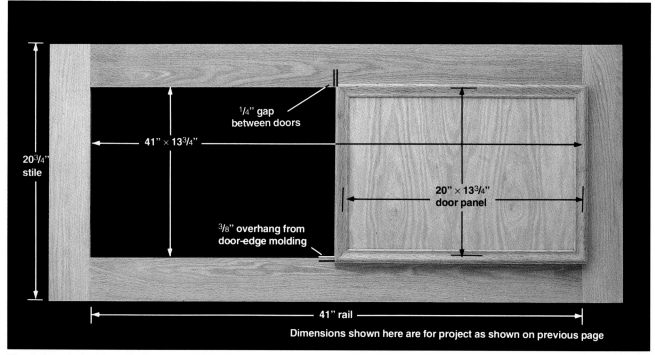

1/4" gap between doors

41" × 13³/₄"

20³/₄" stile

³/₈" overhang from door-edge molding

20" × 13³/₄" door panel

41" rail

Dimensions shown here are for project as shown on previous page

Face frame for the platform bench shown on the previous page is built with 1 × 4 oak stiles and rails joined with blind dowel joints (pages 34 to 35) and installed as one piece. For a good fit, measure and build the face frame after the cabinet is assembled.

Door panels are made from ½" finish-grade plywood and door-edge molding (pages 40 to 43). The panels overlap the face frame by ³/₈", and they are sized to leave a ¼" gap between the doors. Hang the doors with semi-concealed hinges.

How to Build a Platform Bench

1 Measure and mark a level reference line where the top of the platform bench will fit against the wall. Benches installed below a window should be centered with the window.

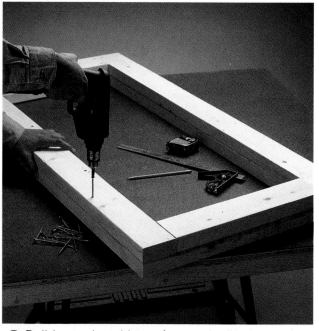

2 Build a pedestal base from a double layer of 2 × 4s, laid flat and joined together with 2¹/2" screws. For greatest pedestal strength, stagger the ends of the 2 × 4s.

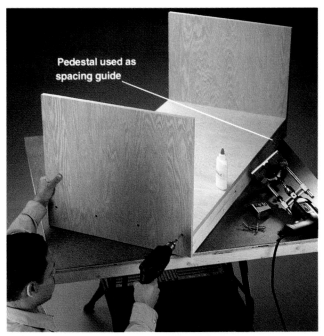

3 Measure and cut a bottom panel (same size as pedestal) and side panels (planned height minus 3/4" for top panel). Rest the bottom panel on the pedestal to achieve proper spacing, then attach the side panels to the base panel, using glue and 2½" screws driven through counterbored pilot holes, at 6" intervals. Do not attach panels to pedestal.

Pedestal used as spacing guide

4 Measure and cut two 2 × 4 supports to the same length as the bottom panel, then clamp the supports together on your workbench, with ends aligned. Cut 1½"-deep, 3½"-wide notches in each 2 × 4, 14" in from each end. Cut notches by making multiple passes using a circular saw with blade set to 1½", then removing the waste wood with a wood chisel.

5 Position the supports at the front and back of the bench cabinet, flush with the tops and sides of the side panels. Drill counterbored pilot holes in the side panels, then attach the supports with glue and 2½" screws.

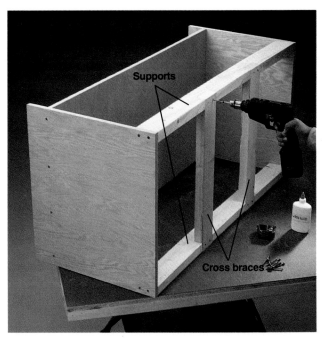

Supports

Cross braces

6 Cut 2 × 4 cross braces the same depth as the base panel. Apply glue to the notches on the supports, then insert the cross braces into the notches and secure them with 2½" screws.

(continued next page)

7 Set the pedestal in the planned location, check to make sure it is level, and shim between the pedestal and the floor if necessary. Anchor the pedestal with 3" screws driven toenail-style into the floor and at shim locations, from inside the pedestal. Trim off shim ends.

8 Set the bench cabinet onto the pedestal, flush against the wall.

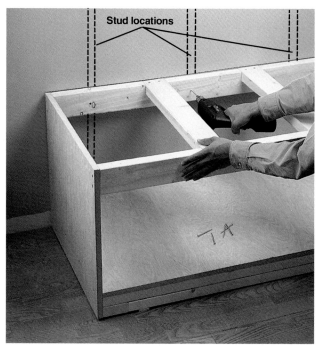

Stud locations

9 Attach the back support of the bench cabinet to the wall with 3" screws driven at wall stud locations, then anchor the bench cabinet to the pedestal by driving 2" screws down through the bottom panel.

10 Measure exact height and length of cabinet and pedestal, then cut 1 × 4 hardwood stiles for face frame, 1/4" shorter than bench height. Cut 1 × 4 rails for face frame, 7" shorter than bench length. Assemble the face frame using blind dowel joints (pages 34 to 35).

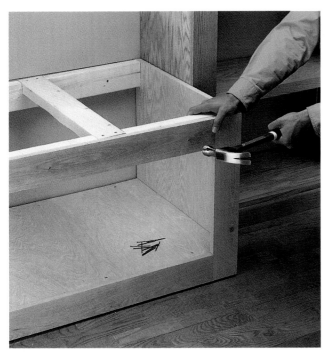

11 Attach the face frame to the front edges of the bench cabinet, using 2" finish nails and glue. The top edge of the bottom face frame rail should be flush with the surface of the bottom panel, leaving a gap above the floor.

12 Build two overlay doors to fit the face frame opening (pages 40 to 43). When determining the size of the door panels, allow for a ¼" gap between the doors after door-edge molding is attached.

13 Attach the doors to the face frame using semi-concealed hinges.

14 Attach magnetic door catches to the top rail of the face frame and to doors, following the manufacturer's directions.

(continued next page)

15 Attach aromatic cedar panels to the inside surfaces of the bench cabinet, or stain and varnish the interior of the cabinet before attaching the top panel.

16 Attach two corner brackets (for anchoring top panel) to the inside face of each side panel, flush with the top edges.

17 Measure and cut a 3/4" oak plywood top panel to fit against the wall and flush with the outside edges of the face frame. Set the top panel in position on the bench cabinet, and attach it from below by driving 1/2" screws through the corner brackets. Drive 2" screws through the 2 × 4 cross braces and into the underside of the top panel.

18 Cover the exposed edges of the top panel with mitered shelf-edge molding. Attach the molding pieces with glue and 1" finish nails driven every 4" to 6" through pilot holes.

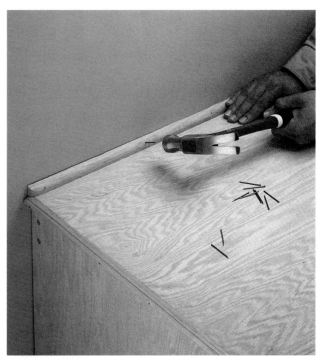

19 Cover gaps between platform bench and floor with mitered base shoe molding, attached with glue and 1" finish nails driven through pilot holes.

20 Cover gaps between platform bench and wall with base shoe molding, attached with glue and 1" finish nails driven through pilot holes.

21 Countersink finish nails with a nail set, and fill all nail and screw holes. Sand and finish the platform bench, then attach door pulls.

Building a Corner Cabinet

See page 13 for more corner cabinet ideas

A desktop and computer desk accessories transform this corner cabinet into a handsome, functional work center. A retractable keyboard shelf supports the keyboard at an easy working height. Computer cables are kept out of sight and tangle-free by a wire organizer. An outlet strip mounted on the desktop is easy to reach and protects the computer from power surges. See pages 48 to 49 for information on electrical accessories.

Most furniture sold in stores does not fit well in a corner. But due to its triangular shape and efficient design, a built-in corner cabinet fits naturally into any room corner.

The corner cabinet featured here includes side panels that make the cabinet deeper. Installed at a right angle to the wall, the side panels also create a good surface for attaching a built-in bookcase.

The corner cabinet as shown was created using dimensions and angles that fit almost any corner, and allow for many uses. For this reason, altering the design is unnecessary and not recommended.

Most tasks in the corner cabinet project can be done with everyday tools, but the long bevel cuts needed for the face frame and side panels are best done with a table saw. If you do not own a table saw, either rent one, or have the cuts made at a woodworking shop.

Due to its size and weight, a corner cabinet should be assembled on-site.

Everything You Need:

Tools: pencil, straightedge, level, handscrew clamps, drill and bits, hammer, jig saw, table saw, utility knife.

Materials: wood glue, finish nails (1", 1½", 2"), power-driver screws (1¼", 1½", 2", 3"), ¾" wire nails, shims, computer desk accessories (photo left, and pages 48 to 49), base shoe molding.

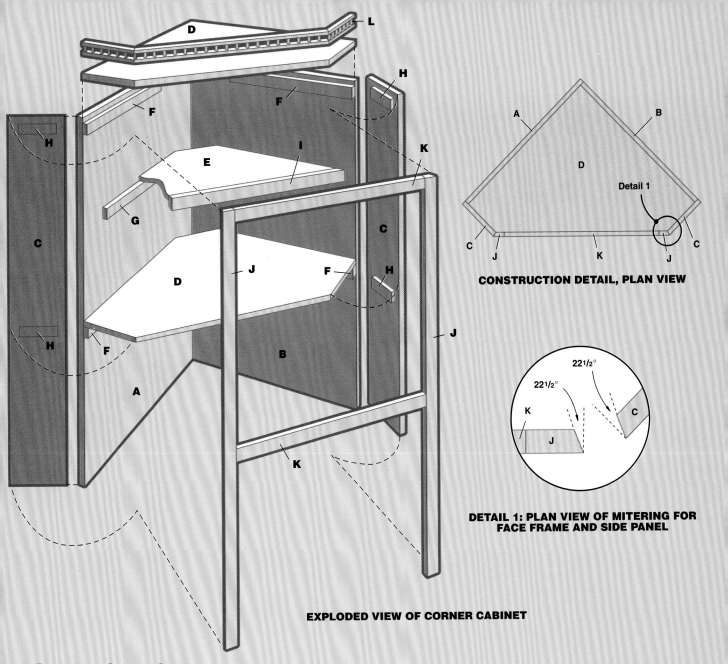

CONSTRUCTION DETAIL, PLAN VIEW

DETAIL 1: PLAN VIEW OF MITERING FOR FACE FRAME AND SIDE PANEL

EXPLODED VIEW OF CORNER CABINET

Parts List: Corner Cabinet

Key	Part	Material	Pieces	Size
A	Left back panel	3/4" oak plywood	1	39" × 66"
B	Right back panel	3/4" oak plywood	1	38 1/4" × 66"
C	Side panels	3/4" oak plywood	2	10" × 66"
D	Desktop and top panel	3/4" oak plywood	2	38 1/4" × 38 1/4" (see detail, page 82)
E	Shelf	3/4" oak plywood	1	34" × 34" (see detail, page 82)
F	Cleats for desktop, top panel	1 × 2	4	31"
G	Cleats for shelf	1 × 2	2	27"
H	Cleats on side panels	1 × 2	4	6"
I	Shelf edging	1 × 2	1	51 1/2"
J	Face frame stiles	1 × 2	2	66"
K	Face frame rails	1 × 2	2	37 1/2"
L	Decorative top trim	spindle rail		5 linear ft.

Corner Cabinet Project Details

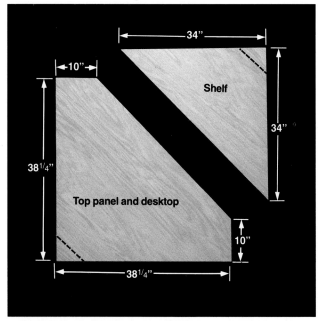

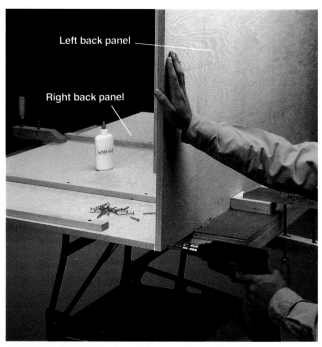

Desktop, top panel, and shelf are made from 3/4" finish-grade plywood. Use a circular saw and a straightedge guide to cut the pieces to the dimensions shown above. If you plan to use the cabinet as a computer work center or an entertainment center, cut off the back corners of the desktop and shelf (but not the top panel) to provide ventilation and space for routing electrical cords.

Back panel and side panels have 1 × 2 hardwood cleats to hold the desktop, shelf, and top panel. Attach them to the panels with glue and 1 1/2" screws driven into counterbored pilot holes. Position cleats according to dimensions shown above. **NOTE:** If you wish to make the shelf the same size as the desktop, add shelf cleats to the side panels (dotted line).

How to Build a Corner Cabinet

1 Measure and cut back panels (left panel overlaps right panel, so it is 3/4" wider than right panel). Cut and attach 1 x 2 cleats according to Project Details (above). Drill counterbored pilot holes in cleats, then attach cleats with glue and 1 1/4" screws.

2 Clamp right back panel (38 1/4" wide) to your workbench, then apply glue to back edge. Butt left panel (39") against glued edge, and hold in place with clamps. Join back panels by drilling pilot holes and driving 2" screws through butt joint.

3 Attach a plastic wire organizer to one back panel edge, next to the corner joint, using 1" wire nails. (Skip this step if you do not plan to store electronic equipment in the corner cabinet.)

4 Measure and cut the desktop (see Project Details, page opposite), then apply glue to the tops of the desktop cleats mounted on the back panels. Set the desktop on the cleats, then attach by drilling pilot holes and driving 1¼" finish nails every 8".

5 Measure and cut shelf (see Project Details), then install on shelf cleats with glue and 1¼" finish nails. Measure and cut a 1 × 2 hardwood shelf edge with 45° mitered corners to fit flush with top of shelf. Attach with 2" finish nails driven through pilot holes.

6 Set a table saw blade to 22½° blade angle, then cut 10"-wide, 66"-long side panels, beveling the front edge of each panel.

7 Attach 6" cleats to side panels (see Project Details) using glue and 1¼" finish nails, then attach side panels to back panels with glue and 1½" screws driven into counterbored pilot holes. Cut top panel (see Project Details) and attach to cleats with 1¼" finish nails.

(continued next page)

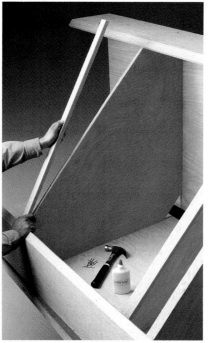

8 With table saw blade set to 22¹/2°, cut 1 × 2 face frame stiles (as in step 6). Apply glue to the outside edge of each side panel, then attach stiles to side panels using 2" finish nails driven through pilot holes at 8" intervals.

9 Measure and cut 1 × 2 face frame rails. Attach them to edges of desktop and top panel, so upper edges of rails are flush with the surfaces of the shelf and top, using glue and 2" finish nails driven through pilot holes.

10 Measure and cut decorative trim to match the angle of the face frame stiles and side panels, then attach the trim to the outside edges at the top of the cabinet, using finish nails.

11 With a helper, move cabinet into corner, flush against the walls.

12 Shim below the side panels, if necessary, to bring the cabinet to level.

13 Drill pilot holes, then toenail the cabinet to the floor at shim locations, using 2" finish nails. Score the shims with a utility knife, then break off the excess shim material.

14 Attach the cabinet to the wall with 3" screws driven through the back panels and into wall studs. Drive screws just behind or below shelf cleats to keep them out of sight.

15 Measure and cut base shoe molding to cover the gap between the cabinet and the walls and floor, using 1¹/₂" finish nails. **TIP:** To protect wall from oil or paint, insert plastic between molding and wall as you attach the molding.

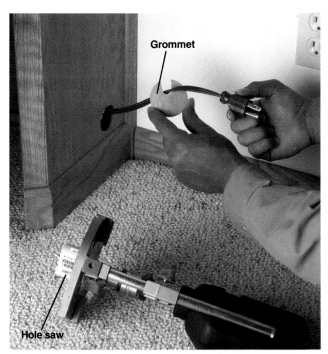

Grommet

Hole saw

16 Sand and finish cabinet, then remove plastic. If cabinet will contain electronic equipment, use a hole saw or forstner bit to cut a hole for an outlet strip cord in side panel, then feed the cord through hole and install a grommet (page 49).

17 Install any other hardware and computer desk accessories, like a retractable keyboard slide, that you need to complete your project (see manufacturer's directions and pages 48 to 49).

Building Basic Cabinets

The simple base cabinet and hanging wall cabinet shown here use the same basic construction as professionally built kitchen cabinets, but because they are custom-designed, trimmed, and finished to blend into the room, they become permanent built-in features of your home.

These basic cabinets are built with oak plywood, which gives them the look of fine custom-made cabinets, but at a much reduced cost. The wall cabinet features glass-panel doors, purchased separately, that create an ideal display area for glassware or china. The base cabinet has extra-large drawers that are well suited for storing table linens.

You can use the methods shown here to build a single base cabinet with a wall cabinet above it, or several cabinets side by side (for a full wall of storage or display).

Everything You Need:

Tools: electronic stud finder, cordless screwdriver, hammer, tape measure, router with bits ($3/4$" straight, $1/4$" rabbet), drill and bits, right-angle drill guide, pegboard scraps, pipe clamps, level.

Materials: power-driver screws ($3/4$", $2^{1}/2$", $3^{1}/2$"), wood glue, finish nails (1", 2", 3", 4"), shims, utility knife, pin-style shelf supports, 2 × 4 brace, 1 × 3 for ledger strip, finishing materials, drawer and door hardware, trim or base shoe molding.

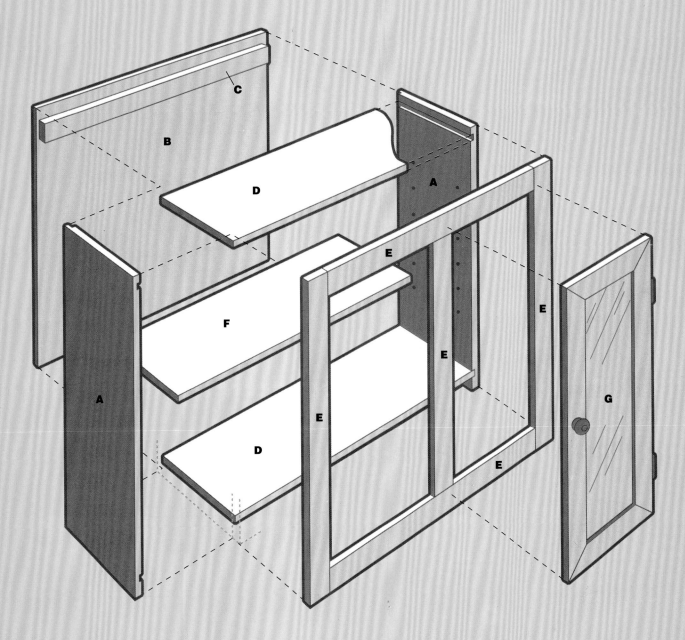

**EXPLODED VIEW OF
HANGING WALL CABINET**

Parts List: Wall Cabinet

	Project as Shown				Your Project	
Key	**Part**	**Material**	**Pieces**	**Size**	**Pieces**	**Size**
A	Side panels	$3/4$" oak plywood	2	$11^{1}/4$" × 30"		
B	Back panel	$1/4$" oak plywood	1	30" × $35^{1}/4$"		
C	Nailing strip	1 × 3 oak	1	$34^{1}/4$"		
D	Top,bottom panels	$3/4$" oak plywood	2	$35^{1}/4$" × $11^{1}/4$"		
E	Face frame	1 × 3 oak	12 linear ft.			
F	Shelves	$3/4$" oak plywood	2	$9^{3}/4$" × $34^{1}/4$"		
G	Glass panel or overlay doors		pages 42 to 43			

Wall Cabinet Project Details

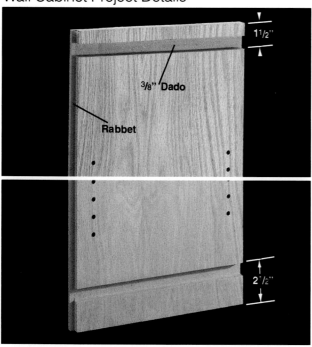

Side panels made from 3/4" plywood have 3/4"-wide, 3/8"-deep dadoes where bottom and top panels will fit and 1/4" wide rabbets where back panel will fit. Rows of parallel peg holes, 11/2" in from edges, will hold pin-style shelf supports.

Back panel made from 1/4" plywood has a 1 × 3 nailing strip mounted 11/2" below top edge of the back panel and set in 3/8" on each side. It is fastened with glue and 3/4" screws driven through the back panel.

How to Build & Install a Wall Cabinet

1 Measure and cut 3/4" plywood side panels, then cut rabbets and dadoes, using a router and a straightedge guide (page 23), following the dimensions in the Project Details (above).

2 Drill two parallel rows of 1/4" holes for pin-style shelf supports on the inside face of each side panel (page 39). Use a right-angle drill guide, and a scrap of pegboard as a template to ensure that holes line up correctly.

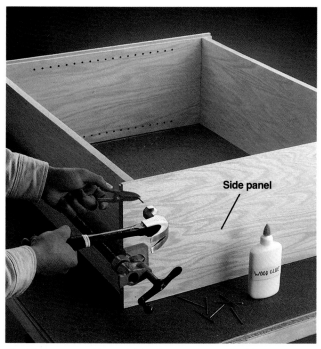

3 Measure and cut 3/4" plywood top and bottom panels, then glue and clamp the side panels to the top and bottom panels to form dado joints (page 33). Reinforce the joints with 2" finish nails driven every 3".

4 Measure, cut, and attach 1 × 3 nailing strip to the back panel (see Project Details), using glue and 3/4" screws. Set the back panel into the rabbets at the back edges of the cabinet. Secure the back with 11/2" wire nails driven into the cabinet edges.

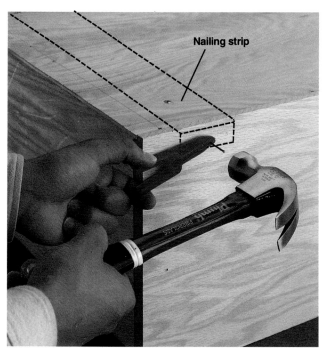

5 Drive 2" finish nails through the side panel and into the ends of the nailing strip.

6 Measure height and width between inside surfaces of cabinet, then cut 1 × 3 face frame rails 43/4" less than the width, and face frame stiles 4" longer than height. Clamp and glue rails between stiles, and reinforce joints by drilling pilot holes and driving 4" finish nails through the stiles into the rails.

(continued next page)

How to Build a Wall Cabinet (continued)

7 Center the face frame on the cabinet so overhang on each side is equal, and top edge of the bottom rail is flush with bottom shelf surface. Attach the face frame with glue and 2" finish nails driven through pilot holes.

8 Fill nail holes, then sand and finish the cabinet.

9 Mark a level reference line on the wall where the bottom edge of the cabinet will be located— 54" above the floor is a standard height. Locate the wall studs, and mark their location below the reference line.

10 Position a temporary 1 × 3 ledger strip so top edge is flush with the reference line, then attach the strip to the wall at stud locations, using 2¹/2" screws.

11 Set cabinet on the temporary ledger, and brace it in position with a 2 × 4. Drill counterbored pilot holes in the nailing strip at the top of the cabinet, and drive 3" screws into wall studs.

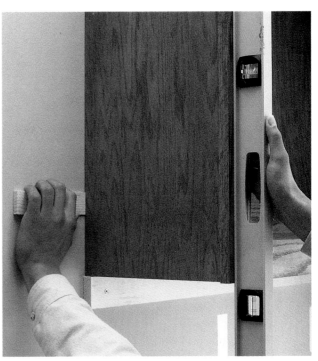

12 Use a level to make sure cabinet is plumb. If not, loosen screws slightly and shim behind the cabinet to adjust it to plumb. Tighten screws completely, then score shims with a utility knife and break off excess.

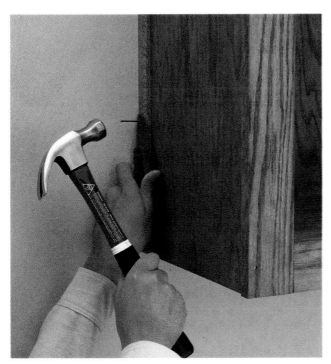

13 Remove temporary ledger and patch screw holes, then cut trim molding to cover gaps between cabinet and the walls. Drill pilot holes and attach trim with 1" finish nails.

14 Build and finish shelves with pin-style shelf supports (pages 38 to 39). Build or purchase overlay doors (pages 40 to 43), and attach them to the face frame. Sand and finish the cabinets, then attach hardware and install shelf support pins and adjustable shelves.

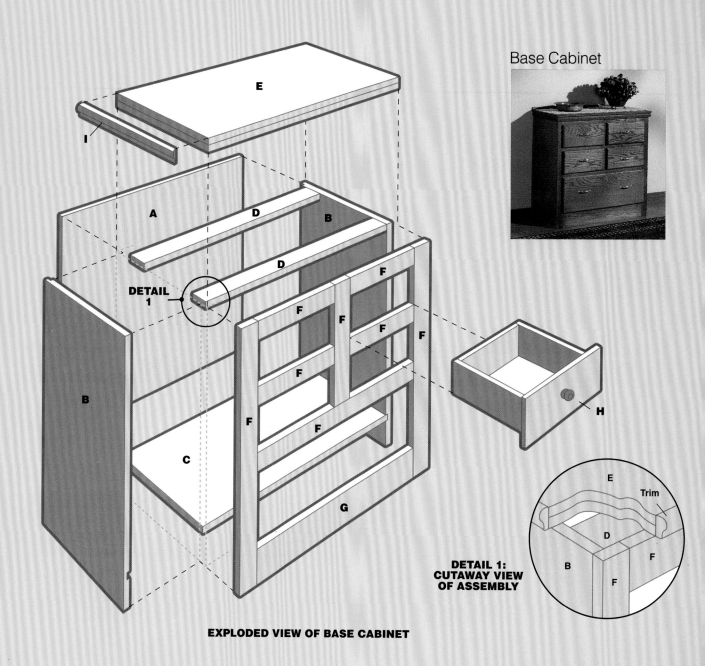

Base Cabinet

EXPLODED VIEW OF BASE CABINET

DETAIL 1
1

**DETAIL 1:
CUTAWAY VIEW
OF ASSEMBLY**

E
Trim
D
B
F
F

Parts List: Base Cabinet

		Project as Shown			Your Project	
Key	**Part**	**Material**	**Pieces**	**Size**	**Pieces**	**Size**
A	Back panel	1/2" plywood	1	34 1/2" × 35 1/4"		
B	Side panels	3/4" plywood	2	34 1/2" × 17 1/4"		
C	Bottom panel	3/4" plywood	1	16 3/4" × 35 1/4"		
D	Supports	1 × 3 oak	2	34 1/2"		
E	Countertop	3/4" plywood	2	36 1/4" × 18"		
F	Face frame	1 × 3 oak		15 linear ft.		
G	Bottom rail	1 × 6 oak	1	31 1/4 "		
H	Overlay drawers			pages 44 to 47		
I	Trim molding			12 linear ft.		

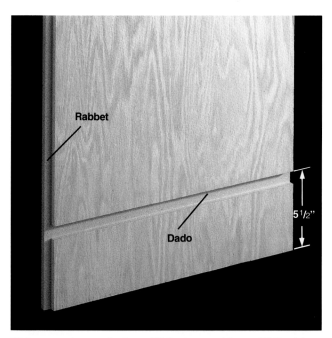

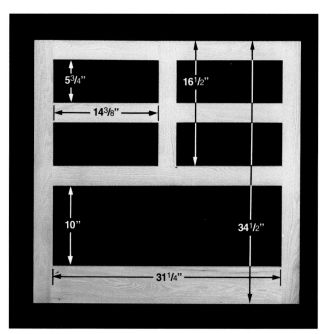

Side panels made from ³/₄" plywood have ³/₄"-wide, ³/₈"-deep dadoes to hold bottom panel, and ¹/₂"-wide, ³/₈"-deep rabbets where back panel will fit. Bottom dado is raised so bottom drawer will be at a comfortable height.

Face frame includes 1 × 6 bottom rails, and 1 × 3s for the stiles and other rails. Cut and assemble face frame, following dimensions shown in photo above.

How to Build & Install a Base Cabinet

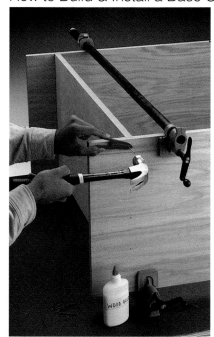

1 Cut ³/₄" plywood side and bottom panels, and ¹/₂" plywood back panel. Cut rabbets and dadoes, following Project Details (above), and assemble the pieces with glue and 2" finish nails, following steps 3 through 5, page 89.

2 Measure, cut, and install two 1 × 3 supports to fit between the side panels at the top of the cabinet. Attach with 2" finish nails driven through the side panels.

3 Measure, cut, and assemble face frame following Project Detail (above), and steps 6 to 7, pages 89 to 90.

(continued next page)

4 Mark location of wall studs in project area, then set cabinet in place. Check with a level and shim under cabinet, if necessary to level it. Toenail the side panels to the floor at shim locations, using 2" finish nails. Score shims, and break off excess.

5 Anchor the cabinet by driving 31/2" screws through the back panel and into wall studs just below the top of the cabinet.

6 Install tracks for two center-mounted drawer slides on the bottom panel (pages 44 to 47).

7 Attach drawer slides for upper drawers to the face frame rails and the back panel, following the manufacturer's directions.

8 Measure and cut two 3/4" plywood countertop panels. Fasten them together with glue and 1" screws driven up through the bottom layer. Set countertop on cabinet, and anchor it with 2" screws driven up through the supports inside the cabinet.

9 Cover exposed edges of countertop with mitered ornamental molding, attached with glue and 2" finish nails driven through pilot holes.

10 Cover gaps between the cabinet and the walls and floor with trim molding, attached with 1" finish nails driven through pilot holes. Finish the cabinet.

11 Build overlay drawers (pages 44 to 47), and finish them to match the cabinet. Install drawers and attach drawer pulls.

See page 14 for more Understairs Work Center ideas

Building an Understairs Work Center

The irregular space beneath a staircase can be used for a variety of creative built-in projects. Because the dimensions and angles of understairs areas vary widely, finding stock cabinetry that fits the space is difficult. But the design shown here can be built to fit almost any area.

The understairs work center, in its simplest form, is a pair of basic cabinets that support a countertop. The basic cabinets are built to a standard height, depending on the use. You can adapt the size of the understairs work center by shortening or lengthening the countertop and connecting shelf. A small cabinet and upper shelves are added to fill out the remaining space. The depth of the countertop also can be adjusted to match the width of your staircase.

Most understairs projects require that you make many angled cuts, but in the project shown here, you will need to make only a few miters and bevels. Beveled cuts can be made with a circular saw, but a table saw is preferable.

Everything You Need:

Tools: pencil, tape measure, level, T-bevel, circular saw or table saw, cordless screwdriver, drill and bits, hammer, router with 3/4" straight bit and 3/8" rabbet bit, bar clamps, miter saw.

Materials: shims, finish nails (1", 1 1/4", 2"), power-driver screws (1", 1 1/4", 2 1/2"), 1" wire nails, trim molding, finishing materials, door and drawer hardware.

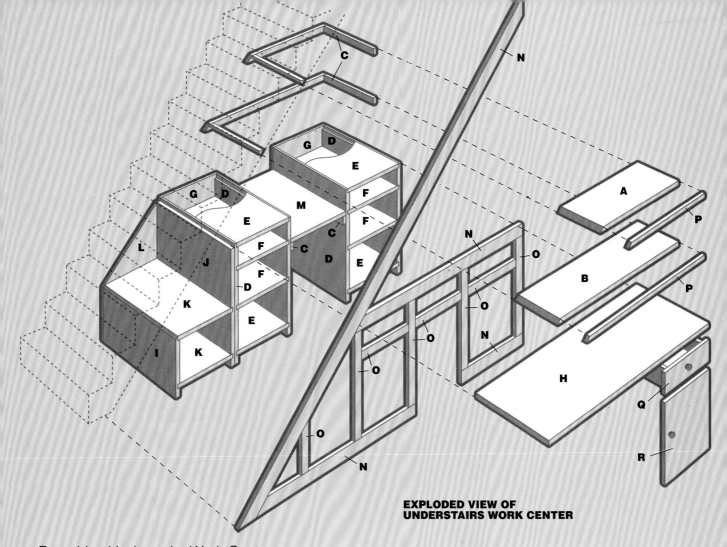

**EXPLODED VIEW OF
UNDERSTAIRS WORK CENTER**

Parts List: Understairs Work Center

		Project as Shown			Your Project	
Key	**Part**	**Material**	**Pieces**	**Size**	**Pieces**	**Size**
A	Top shelf	$^3/4$" plywood	1	28" × 18"		
B	Lower shelf	$^3/4$" plywood	1	42" × 18"		
C	Shelf cleats	1 × 2	12 linear ft.			
D	Cabinet sides	$^3/4$" plywood	4	$35^1/2$" × 24"		
E	Cabinet base, top panels	$^3/4$" plywood	4	24" × $19^1/4$"		
F	Cabinet shelves	$^3/4$" plywood	4	24" × $19^1/4$"		
G	Cabinet backs	$^1/4$" plywood	2	20" × 35"		
H	Countertop	$^3/4$" plywood	1	32" × 64"		
I	Small cabinet side	$^3/4$" plywood	1	18" × 24"		
J	Small cabinet side	$^3/4$" plywood	1	$34^1/2$" × 24"		
K	Small cabinet bottom & top	$^3/4$" plywood	2	$19^1/4$" × 24"		
L	Small cabinet back	$^1/4$" plywood	1	20" × 34"		
M	Connecting shelf	$^3/4$" plywood	1	$27^7/8$" × 24"		
N	Face frame pieces	1 × 3 oak	26 linear ft.			
O	Face frame pieces	1 × 2 oak	25 linear ft.			
P	Shelf edge strips	$^3/4$" hardwood	4 linear ft.			
Q	Drawers	see pages 44 to 47				
R	Cabinet doors	see pages 40 to 43				

Underststairs Work Center Project Details

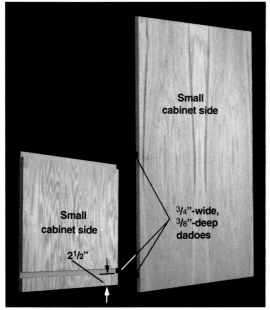

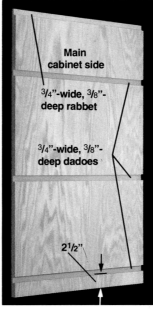

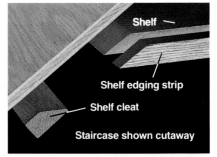

Small cabinet side

Small cabinet side

3/4"-wide, 3/8"-deep dadoes

2¹/2"

Main cabinet side

3/4"-wide, 3/8"-deep rabbet

3/4"-wide, 3/8"-deep dadoes

2¹/2"

Shelf —

Shelf edging strip

Shelf cleat

Staircase shown cutaway

Side panels for short cabinet (left), made from 3/4" plywood, differ in size. A line connecting the tops of the two panels should follow the slope line of the staircase. **Side panels for main cabinets (right),** also made from 3/4" plywood, have dadoes for the cabinet shelves and base, and rabbets for the cabinet top. The taller side panel for the small cabinet fits against a main cabinet side panel when the work center is installed.

Shelves and cleats, made from plywood and 1 × 2 strips, are beveled so they fit flush against the understairs cover. The shelf edging strips are cut from oak 1 × 2, and mitered at the same angle as the shelves.

Tips for Building an Understairs Work Center

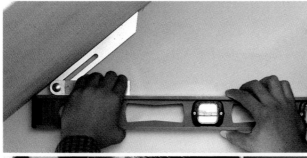

Duplicate the slope of your stairs using a T-bevel. Set one arm of the T-bevel in a level position against the back wall, then align the other arm with the stairs (top photo). Transfer the angle directly to your saw to make mitered and beveled cuts (bottom photo).

Cover stair underside before you install your understairs work center. Panels of 1/2" plywood attached to the stringers of the staircase create an understairs cover that can be used to anchor shelf cleats. If you plan to add electrical or plumbing lines, do the work (or hire a professional if you are inexperienced) before installing your built-in.

How to Build an Understairs Work Center

1 Mark the location for the shelf cleats on the walls and understairs cover, using a level as a guide. Butt the 12" cleats against the back wall, and allow at least 12" of clearance between the countertop and the bottom shelf.

2 Measure and cut 1 × 2 shelf cleats to fit along the reference lines on the walls and the understairs cover (see Project Details, page opposite). Bevel the cleats on the understairs cover to match the stair slope angle. Attach the cleats with 2 1/2" screws.

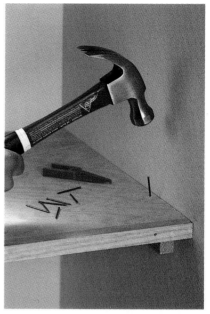

3 Measure and cut 3/4" plywood shelves, then attach a 3/4" hardwood strip to each shelf edge (see Project Details, page opposite) using glue and finish nails. Set shelves on cleats and attach with 1 1/2" finish nails driven through pilot holes.

4 Measure and cut 3/4" plywood side panels for main cabinets, then use a router and straightedge guide (page 23) to cut rabbets for top panels and dadoes for bottom panels and shelves (see Project Details, page opposite).

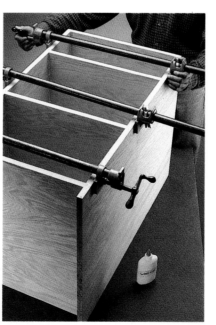

5 Clamp and glue the cabinet sides to the top and bottom panels and shelves to form rabbet and dado joints. **NOTE:** If you plan to install center-mounted drawer slides, mount slide tracks before you assemble the cabinet.

6 Reinforce each cabinet joint with 2" finish nails driven at 4" intervals.

(continued next page)

7 Cut a 1/4" plywood back panel for each main cabinet. Set each back onto a cabinet frame so all sides align, then attach to cabinet side, base, and top panels using 1" wire nails.

8 Position one cabinet so top panel is pressed against the understairs cover and front face is flush with edge of stairway. Shim if needed, then toenail into the floor through the side panels, using 2" finish nails. For masonry floors, attach with construction adhesive.

9 Position other cabinet 3/4" away from side wall, with front face aligned with first cabinet. Check with a level and shim if needed. Insert 3/4" spacers between cabinet and side wall, then anchor to wall with 2 1/2" screws driven into framing members.

10 Cut 1 × 2 cleats for the connecting shelf that fits between the main cabinets. Mark level lines on the inner cabinet sides, then attach shelf cleats to the cabinet sides by driving 1 1/4" screws through counterbored pilot holes.

11 Measure and cut a 3/4" plywood connecting shelf to fit between the cabinets, and attach it to the cleats with 1 1/4" finish nails. (If you plan to build a drawer using a center-mounted drawer slide, attach the slide track to the shelf before you attach the shelf to the cleats.)

12 Measure and cut a plywood countertop panel that extends all the way to the back wall, with one side flush against the understairs cover. Attach the countertop to top panels of cabinets by driving 1¹/2" finish nails down through the countertop.

13 Apply or install any special countertop finishing material, like ceramic tile or plastic laminate. Obtain installation instructions and follow them carefully if you have not installed tile or laminate before.

Back panel

Top panel

Side panel

14 Build a small cabinet the same width and depth as the main cabinets (steps 4 to 7). Adjust the height of the side panels to follow the stair slope (see Project Details, page 98). Cut a ¼" plywood back panel, with the top edge sloped at the same angle as the line between the side panel tops. Attach the back panel to the cabinet with 1" wire nails.

15 Position the small cabinet so the taller side panel is flush against the main cabinet. Align the face of the small cabinet with the face of the main cabinet, then check with a level, and shim if necessary. Connect the cabinets by drilling pilot holes, and driving 1¹/4" screws through the side panels.

(continued next page)

If corners are open at top and bottom of stairs, attach nailing strips to the understairs cover and cabinet sides, then cut 1/2" plywood panels to fit the space, and attach them to the nailing strips with 1" screws.

16 Measure and cut 1 × 3 bottom rails for the cabinets. Also cut a long, diagonal rail to fit along the edge of the understairs cover. Miter the ends of the diagonal rail to fit against the floor and the side wall, and miter the longer bottom rail to form a clean joint with the diagonal rail. Test-fit the rails, then attach them with glue and 2" finish nails driven through pilot holes.

17 Measure and cut 1 × 3 rails to cover the edges of the connecting shelf and the countertop. Miter the end of the countertop rail that joins the long, diagonal rail. Attach the shelf and countertop rails flush with the countertop and shelf surfaces, using glue and 2" nails driven through pilot holes.

18 Measure and cut 1 × 2 stiles for the front edges of the cabinets. Attach the stiles, flush with the edges of the cabinet sides, using glue and 2" nails driven through pilot holes.

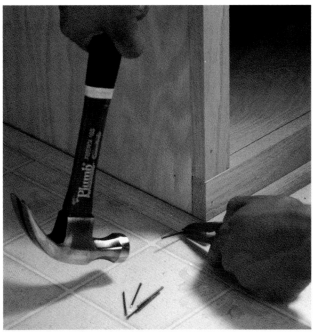

19 Measure and cut 1 × 2 rails to fit between the stiles, so they cover the cabinet shelf edges and are flush with the shelf tops. Attach the rails, using glue and 2" nails driven through pilot holes.

20 Cut base-shoe molding to cover gaps along wall and floor surfaces, mitering the corners. Attach molding, using 1" finish nails. Sand, fill, and finish the understairs center.

21 Attach slide tracks for side-mounted drawer slides, according to the manufacturer's directions.

22 Build, finish, and install drawers (see pages 44 to 47) and drawer hardware. Purchase or build and finish cabinet doors (pages 40 to 43), then hang doors using ⅜" semi-concealed hinges.

Building a Room Divider

A room divider, like a partition wall, separates one large room into two usable spaces, each with its own specific function. But unlike a partition wall, a room divider adds storage space to your home, while letting you retain the open feeling of a larger room.

Room dividers commonly are used to separate a large kitchen/dining area into two different "rooms." Adding a pass-through and overhanging countertop, as in the project shown here, creates a casual dining area.

In the design featured here, the room divider is built in two main sections: the base cabinet with countertop, and the upper shelf unit. The two sections are joined by a floor-to-ceiling plywood framework to create one attractive unit.

A room divider lends itself to personal touches, like mounting a wine rack and stemware racks on the underside of the shelf unit to make a convenient dry bar.

Everything You Need:

Tools: stepladder, pencil, level, tape measure, plumb bob, framing square, router with 3/4" straight bit, circular saw or table saw, handscrew clamps, bar clamps, drill and bits, screwdriver, hammer, nail set, putty knife.

Materials: wood glue, finish nails (1", 1 1/4", 2"), power-driver screws (1", 1 1/4", 2", 2 1/2", 3"), shims, 3/4" hardwood strips, countertop trim, shelf-edge trim, pin-style shelf supports, finishing materials, door hardware.

An overhanging countertop gives this room divider an added dimension as a convenient dining surface located near the food preparation area of the kitchen. The cabinets on the kitchen side of the room divider also provide accessible storage space for pots, pans, and kitchenware. The open shelves in the upper half of the room divider are ideal for displaying glassware or collectibles.

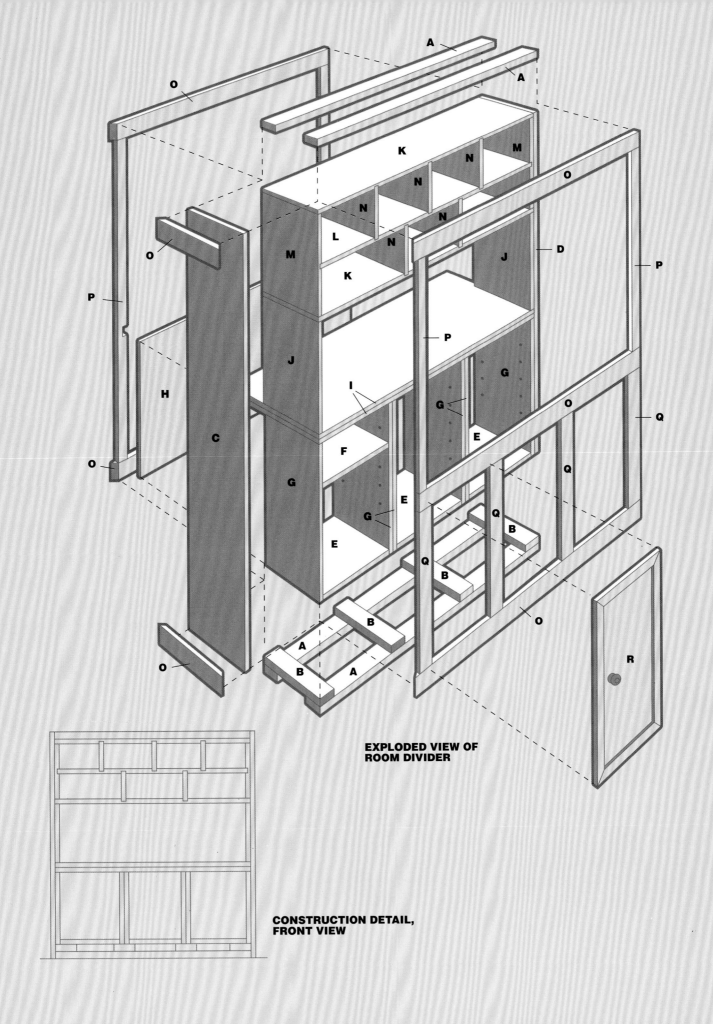

EXPLODED VIEW OF ROOM DIVIDER

CONSTRUCTION DETAIL, FRONT VIEW

Parts List: Room Divider

		Project as Shown				Your Project	
Key	Part	Material	Pieces	Size		Pieces	Size
A	Top and sole plates	2 × 4	4	71$\frac{1}{4}$"			
B	Sole plate cross braces	2 × 4	4	15"			
C	Outer end panel	3/4" oak plywood	1	95$\frac{1}{2}$" × 15"			
D	Inner end panel	3/4" oak plywood	1	91" × 15"			
E	Base panels	3/4"oak plywood	3	22" × 14$\frac{3}{4}$"			
F	Cabinet shelves	3/4"oak plywood	3	21$\frac{3}{4}$" × 14$\frac{3}{4}$"			
G	Cabinet risers	3/4" oak plywood	6	30" × 14$\frac{3}{4}$"			
H	Cabinet back panel	1/4" oak plywood	1	32" × 70"			
I	Countertop panels	3/4" oak plywood	2	70$\frac{1}{2}$" × 24"			
J	Shelf unit supports	3/4" oak plywood	2	33" × 15"			
K	Top, bottom shelf panels	3/4" oak plywood	2	70$\frac{1}{2}$" × 15"			
L	Center shelf panel	3/4" oak plywood	1	69$\frac{3}{4}$" × 15"			
M	Shelf unit sides	3/4" oak plywood	2	25$\frac{1}{2}$" × 15"			
N	Shelf unit risers	3/4" oak plywood	5	12$\frac{1}{2}$" × 15"			
O	Face frame rails	1 × 4 oak	33 linear ft.				
P	Face frame stiles	1 × 2 oak	26 linear ft.				
Q	Face frame stiles	1 × 3 oak	12 linear ft.				
R	Overlay doors	see pages 40 to 43					

Room Divider Project Details

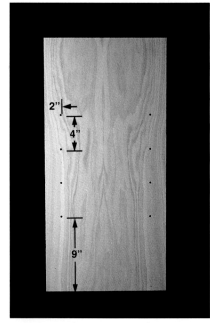

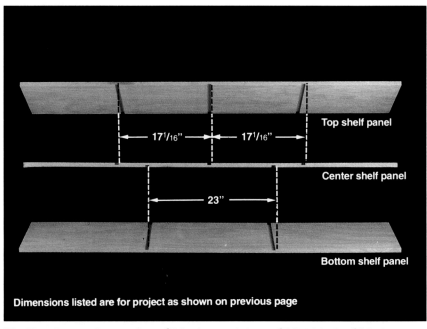

Dimensions listed are for project as shown on previous page

Cabinet risers, cut from 3/4" plywood, have holes for pin-style shelf supports drilled at 4" intervals, 2" in from edges of each riser face. Holes start 9" from top and bottom.

Shelf-unit panels, cut from 3/4" plywood, have 3/4"-wide by 3/8"-deep dadoes to hold the shelf risers. The center shelf panel is dadoed on both the top and the bottom faces, and the top and bottom shelf panels are dadoed on one face only.

How to Build a Room Divider

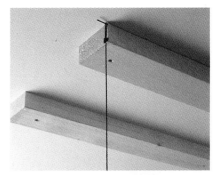

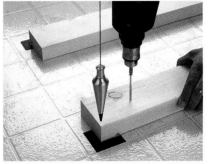

1 Mark the location for the top plates on the ceiling, using a framing square to ensure that lines are perpendicular to the wall. Locate wall studs and ceiling joists in the project area, and install blocking if necessary (page 29).

2 Cut two 2 × 4 top plates and position them against the ceiling, with the outside edges flush against the reference lines. Check to see if plates are level, and install shims if needed. Anchor plates to ceiling joists or blocking, using 3" screws.

3 Cut two 2 × 4 sole plates, and align them directly under the top plates, using a plumb bob as a guide. Check to see if plates are level, shim if needed, then anchor the sole plates to the floor, using 3" screws.

4 Cut and attach 2 × 4 cross braces across the sole plates, using 2¹/2" screws. Position the cross braces at the ends of the sole plates, and below the planned cabinet riser locations.

5 Measure and cut the outer end panel ¹/2" shorter than the floor-to-ceiling height to allow for adjustments. Align end panel with the edges of the 2 × 4 plates, then attach it to the top and sole plates, using 2¹/2" screws driven into counterbored pilot holes.

(continued next page)

6 Measure and cut the inner end panel 1/2" shorter than the distance between the top plate and sole plate cross braces, and slide it in place. Align the panel with the edges of the top plate and sole plate cross braces, then attach it to the wall with 2¹/2" screws driven into wall studs or blocking.

7 Measure and cut plywood cabinet risers with holes for shelf supports (see Project Details, page 106). Risers should be ¼" narrower than end panels, and 1½" shorter than the distance from sole plate cross braces to planned countertop height. Attach a riser to each end panel, flush with the front edge, by driving 1¼" screws through counterbored pilot holes.

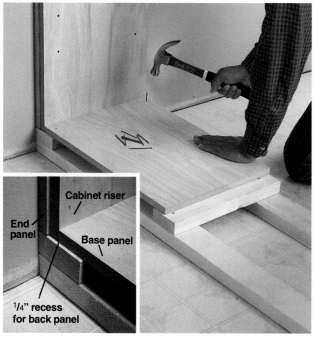

8 Measure and cut plywood base panels the same width as the risers. Lay one base panel across the sole plate cross braces, butted against the riser at the inner end panel, with the 1/4" recess at the back side (inset). Attach the base panel, using 2" finish nails.

9 Make riser assemblies (for inner riser locations) by joining two risers together, back-to-back, with glue and 1¹/4" finish nails. Set one riser assembly on the cross brace next to the first base panel, and attach it with 2¹/2" screws driven through pilot holes and into the base panel edge.

10 Install the middle base panel, then the second riser assembly, then the last base panel, using the techniques shown in steps 8 to 9.

11 Measure and cut two plywood countertop panels, 24" wide, to fit between the end panels, and set the first panel on the cabinet risers, flush with the front edges of the end panels. Use a framing square to adjust the risers so they are perpendicular to the countertop, then drill pilot holes and drive $2^1/2$" screws through countertop and into risers.

12 Apply glue to the top of the first countertop panel, then set the second countertop panel on the first panel. Clamp the panels together, then join them by driving 1" screws up through the underside of the first panel.

13 Measure and cut a $1/4$" oak plywood back panel to fit into the recess created by the back edges of the risers and base panels (see step 8). Set the back panel into the recess, then attach it to the cabinet risers and base panels, using 1" wire nails driven at 8" intervals.

(continued next page)

14 Measure and cut plywood shelf panels for the upper shelf unit, then cut ¾"-wide, ⅜"-deep dadoes at shelf riser locations (see Project Details, page 106). **TIP:** "Gang-cut" dadoes to speed up your work: mark locations for dado cuts on panels, then clamp them together so dado marks align.

15 Measure and cut plywood shelf unit sides. Make a 3/4"-wide, 3/8"-deep dado in each side, where the center shelf panel will fit.

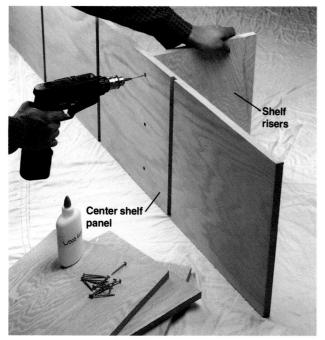

16 Measure and cut plywood shelf unit risers the same width as the center shelf. Stand the center shelf panel on its side, then glue the shelf risers into dadoes. Reinforce the joints with 2" screws driven into counterbored pilot holes.

17 Assemble the remaining pieces of the upper shelf unit, using glue and 2" screws driven into counterbored pilot holes. Attach side panels to center shelf, then attach top and bottom shelf panels to side panel and shelf risers. Make sure diagonal measurements of shelf unit are equal (if not, adjust unit as needed until it is square).

18 Measure and cut plywood shelf unit supports. Supports should be tall enough to leave a gap of about 1" beneath the top plates when the shelf unit is mounted on their top edges. Attach the shelf unit supports to the inner and outer end panels, using glue and 1¹/4" finish nails.

19 With a helper, lift the shelf unit onto the tops of the shelf unit supports. There should be a gap of about 1" between the shelf unit and the top plates.

20 Align the edges of the upper shelf unit with the edges of the end panels. Attach the shelf unit by driving 1¹/4" finish nails through the side panels and into the end panels. Space nails 4" apart, along outer edges of shelf unit.

21 Set a 2 × 4 brace between the countertop and the shelf unit, then measure and cut 1 × 4 top and bottom rails for the face frames. Miter the corner joints at the edges of the outer end panel, and butt the trim against the wall at the inner end panel. Drill pilot holes, and attach rails with glue and 2" finish nails driven into panels and framing members.

(continued next page)

22 Measure and cut 1 × 4 countertop rail to reach from the wall to the outside edge of the outer end panel, on the front side of the room divider. Attach the rail to the edge of the countertop, using glue and 2" finish nails driven through pilot holes.

23 Measure and cut 1 × 2 face frame stiles to fit between the bottom rail and the top rail at the back of the room divider. Make a 3/4" × 1 1/2" notch in each stile, where the edge of the countertop will fit. Attach the stiles to the end panels, using glue and 2" finish nails driven through pilot holes.

24 Measure and cut 1 × 2 stiles to fit between the countertop rail and the top rail at the front of the room divider. Position stiles over the edges of the end panel, and attach with glue and 2" finish nails driven through pilot holes.

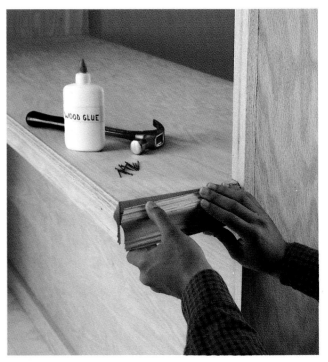

25 Cover the countertop overhang with ornamental trim molding mitered at a 45° angle at corner joints. Attach with glue and 1 1/2" finish nails driven through pilot holes.

26 Measure and cut 1 × 3 stiles to fit between the bottom rail and the countertop rail on the back side of the room divider. Position end stiles flush with the outside faces of the end panels, and center the interior stiles over the riser assemblies. Attach with glue and 2" finish nails driven through pilot holes.

27 Attach ³/₄" shelf-edge strips to all exposed edges of the upper shelf unit, using glue and 1" finish nails driven through pilot holes. Cut horizontal strips the full length of the shelf unit, then add vertical strips between the horizontal strips.

28 Cut adjustable shelves for the cabinets, attach shelf-edge trim if desired, then install shelves, using pin-style shelf supports (pages 38 to 39).

29 Cover gaps at ceiling with cove molding, and along floor and wall with base shoe molding. Fill holes, sand, then apply finish. Build, finish, and hang overlay cabinet doors (pages 40 to 43). Attach all remaining hardware.

Building an Entertainment Center

This handsome and unique entertainment center provides ample storage for all your home electronics, yet is relatively compact—5 ft. high and less than 7 ft. wide. The three-unit design features a 20"-deep center unit spacious enough to hold a large television set, and two 16"-deep end units ideal for storing stereo speakers, tapes, CDs, and books.

Because the project is built in three units, it is easy to adapt. For example, you might choose to expand the project by building additional end units to occupy a long wall. Or, for a small room you might choose to build only the center unit. You also can change the width of the center unit to match the size of your television set.

Everything You Need:

Tools: tape measure, circular saw, straight-edge guide, pencil, router and bits (¾" rabbet, ¾" straight), hammer, drill and bits, power screwdriver, right-angle drill guide, pegboard scraps, miter saw, jig saw, bar clamps, utility knife.

Materials: masking tape, finish nails (1¼", 2"), wood glue, 1" wire nails, shims, power-driver screws (1", 3"), ¼" oak plywood for top cover, ¾" wire brads, electrical accessories (pages 48 to 49), drawer and door hardware, finishing materials, base shoe molding.

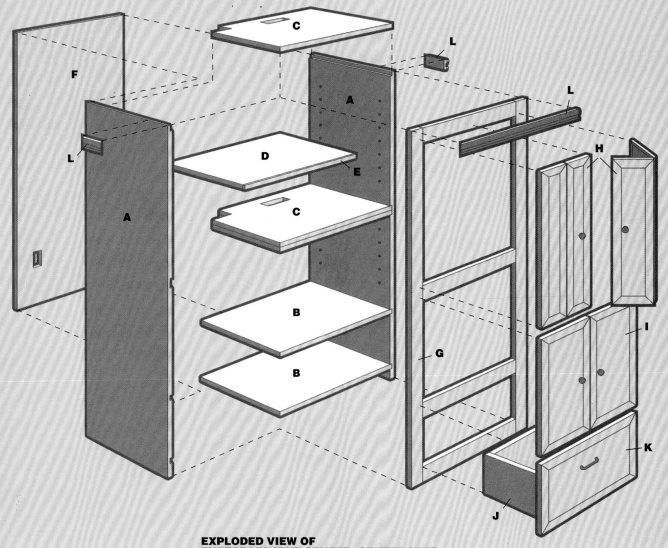

**EXPLODED VIEW OF
ENTERTAINMENT CENTER, CENTER UNIT**

Parts List: Center Unit

Project as Shown					Your Project	
Key	**Part**	**Material**	**Pieces**	**Size**	**Pieces**	**Size**
A	Side panels	3/4" oak plywood	2	20" × 60"		
B	Bottom panels	3/4" oak plywood	2	20" × 31 1/4"		
C	Permanent shelves	3/4" oak plywood	3	20" × 31 1/4"		
D	Adjustable shelves	3/4" oak plywood	2	19 1/2" × 30 1/4"		
E	Shelf edges	Shelf-edge molding	31 linear ft.			
F	Back panel	1/2" oak plywood	1	32" × 60"		
G	Face frame	1 × 3	23 linear ft.			
H	Folding door panels	1/2" oak plywood	4	6" × 23 1/2"		
I	Overlay doors		pages 40 to 43			
J	Overlay drawer		pages 44 to 47			
K	Drawer face	1/2" oak plywood	1	9" × 27"		
L	Top trim	Ornamental molding	6 linear ft.			

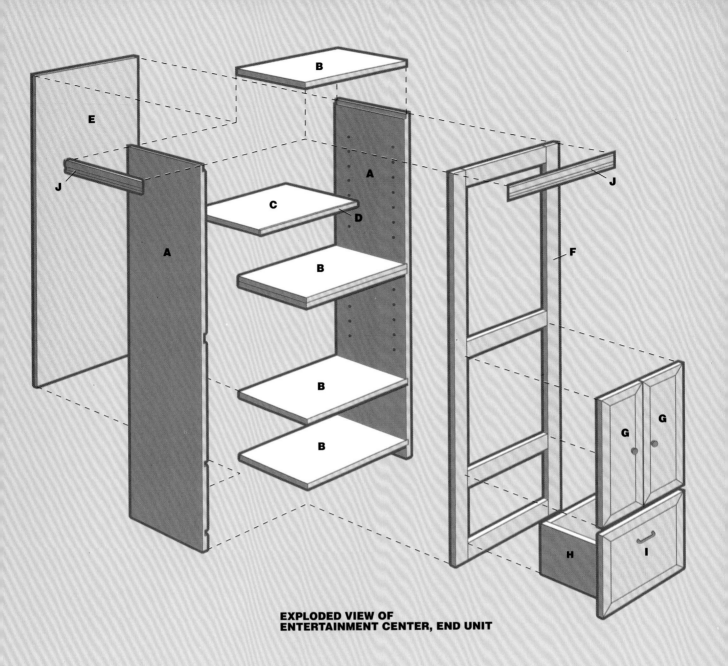

**EXPLODED VIEW OF
ENTERTAINMENT CENTER, END UNIT**

Parts List: For Each End Unit

Project as Shown					Your Project	
Key	**Part**	**Material**	**Pieces**	**Size**	**Pieces**	**Size**
A	Side panels	3/4" oak plywood	2	16" × 60"		
B	Fixed shelves	3/4" oak plywood	5	16" × 23 1/4"		
C	Adjustable shelves	3/4" oak plywood	2	15 1/2" × 22 1/4"		
D	Shelf-edges	Shelf-edge molding	2	22 1/4"		
E	Back panel	1/2" oak plywood	1	24" × 60"		
F	Face frame	1 × 3	20 linear ft.			
G	Overlay doors	pages 40 to 43				
H	Overlay drawer	pages 44 to 47				
I	Drawer face	1/2" oak plywood	1	9" × 22"		
J	Top trim	Ornamental molding	3 linear ft.			

Entertainment Center Project Details

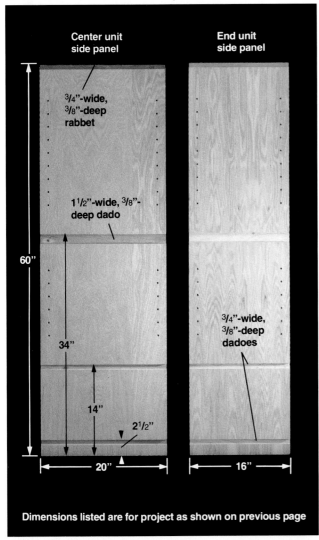

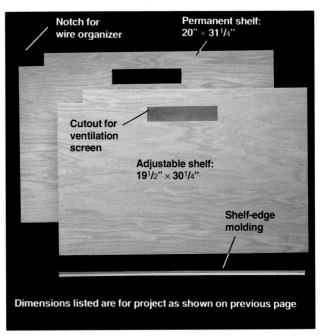

Center unit shelves (above) made from 3/4" plywood have notches cut in the back corner to accommodate a vertical wire organizer track, and cutouts sized to hold ventilation screens. Adjustable shelves are faced with shelf-edge molding.

Side panels (left) for center unit and end unit are made from 3/4" plywood, and differ only in width. Dadoes and rabbets will hold the top panel, bottom panel, and permanent shelves. Parallel rows of peg holes, drilled 2" from front and back edges and beginning 4 1/2" above permanent shelves, will hold pin-style supports for the adjustable shelves.

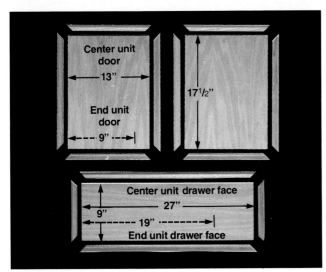

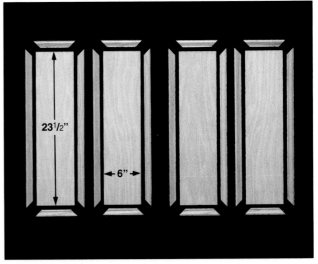

Drawer faces & overlay doors are built with 1/2" plywood framed with mitered door-edge molding. Doors and drawers for end units are the same height as those for the center unit, but are not as wide.

Folding doors for center unit are made of 1/2" plywood panels, framed on all sides by mitered door-edge molding. Two butt hinges join each pair of framed panels.

How to Build an Entertainment Center

1 Remove baseboards and other moldings, then mark the planned location of the entertainment center on the floor, using masking tape. **NOTE:** Back panel of the entertainment center can be cut out to provide access to a wall receptacle located in the project area.

2 Measure and cut 3/4" plywood side panels for the center unit, using a circular saw and a straight-edge guide (page 23).

3 Cut rabbets and dadoes (page 33) in the side panels at the locations shown in the Project Details (page 117), using a router and two straight-edge guides.

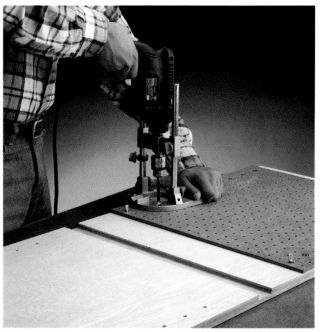

4 Drill two vertical rows of 1/4" holes along the inside face of each side panel to hold pin-style shelf supports. Use a right-angle drill guide, and a pegboard scrap as a template to ensure that holes are aligned correctly (page 39). Holes should be drilled 2" from the edges of the panels.

5 Measure and cut ¾" plywood permanent shelves and adjustable shelves. Use a jig saw to cut corner notches where wire organizer will fit, and to make cutouts for ventilation screens (see Project Details, page 117).

6 Join two of the notched permanent shelves together with glue and 1¼" finish nails to form one double-layer shelf for the middle of the center unit.

7 Measure and cut shelf-edge molding to cover the exposed front edges of the adjustable shelves. Glue and clamp the molding to the shelves, then drill pilot holes and drive 1¼" finish nails through the molding and into the shelves.

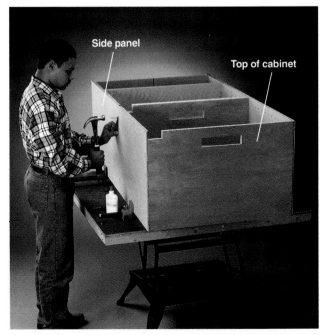

8 Measure and cut ¾" plywood bottom panels, then attach the track for a center-mounted drawer slide at the center of one of the bottom panels (pages 44 to 47).

9 Glue and clamp the bottom panels and permanent shelves between the side panels to form dado and rabbet joints. Reinforce each joint with 2" finish nails driven 4" to 6" apart.

(continued next page)

10 Measure and cut 1/2" plywood back panel, then tack a 30" wire organizer track 1" from the edge of the panel, along the side where the notches will be located.

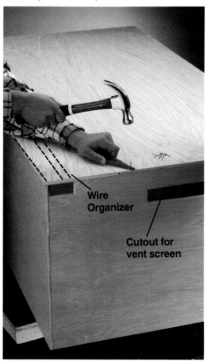

Wire Organizer

Cutout for vent screen

11 Position the back panel over the back of the center unit so edges are flush. Attach it by driving wire nails every 4" into the shelves and side panels.

12 If cabinet will cover a wall receptacle, make a cutout in the back panel, slightly larger than the coverplate, to provide access to the receptacle.

13 Position the center unit against the wall inside the floor outline. Check with a level, and shim under the sides of the center unit, if necessary, until it is level and plumb. Score shims with a utility knife, and snap off the excess.

14 Measure, cut, and prepare side panels, permanent shelves, and back panels for each end unit (see Project Details, page 117), then assemble the pieces, following steps 2 to 9.

15 Position the end units next to the center unit. If necessary, shim under the side panels to align the tops of the end units with the center unit.

16 Join each end unit to the center unit by drilling counterbored pilot holes and driving 1" screws through the side panels and into the center unit.

17 Anchor the center unit and end units to the wall by drilling counterbored pilot holes and driving 3" screws through the back panels and into the wall at stud locations.

18 Measure and cut 1 × 2 vertical face frame stiles and attach them to the center unit and end units, using glue and finish nails driven through pilot holes. Edges of stiles should be flush with outside edges of the side panels.

(continued next page)

19 Cut 1 × 3 horizontal face frame rails to fit between the stiles, along the edges of the permanent shelves and bottom panels. Attach them with glue and 2" finish nails, so upper edges of the rails are flush with the top surfaces of the shelves and bottom panels. Anchor the rails to the stiles by drilling pilot holes and driving 2" finish nails diagonally through the rails and into the stiles (inset).

20 Lay a sheet of 1/4" oak plywood on the entertainment center, and outline the top of the entertainment center onto the plywood. Also mark cutouts for the wire organizer notch and ventilation screen. Cut the plywood along the marked lines, using a jig saw, then attach it to the top of the entertainment center with 3/4" wire brads.

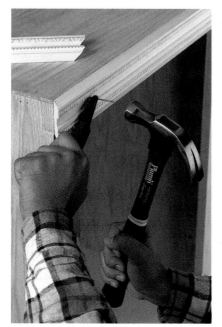

21 Trim the top of the entertainment center with mitered ornamental molding to cover the exposed edges of the plywood. Attach the moldings by drilling pilot holes and driving 1 1/4" finish nails into the top rails and side panels.

22 Cover gaps along the wall and floor with base shoe molding, attached with 1" finish nails driven through pilot holes.

23 Fill and plug the nail and screw holes, then sand and finish the entertainment center.

24 Insert ventilation screens into the cutouts in the shelf panels, then attach an electrical outlet strip to the back panel on the center cabinet, just above the double-layer middle shelf.

25 If you need to run wires between units, cut holes through side panels, using a hole saw or forstner bit, and install grommets.

26 Build folding overlay doors for center unit by framing two pairs of ½" plywood panels with door-edge molding (see Project Details, page 117). Finish doors to match entertainment center, then join each pair with butt hinges attached to backs of panels.

27 Mount the folding doors to the center unit face frame with semi-concealed hinges (pages 40 to 43).

28 Build, finish, and install remaining overlay doors (pages 40 to 43) and drawers (pages 44 to 47) for the center unit and end unit. (**NOTE:** The drawer design for this project varies slightly from standard design by using framed plywood panels, not solid hardwood, for the drawer faces). Attach drawer pulls and doorknobs.

Selecting a Finish

A good finish both protects and beautifies wood. To achieve both goals, a finish is made up of several layers, each with its own specific purpose. Each element of a finish should be chosen carefully, according to the features of the wood, the function of the project piece, and your tastes.

On a new wood, apply a seal coat made of sanding sealer to create more even finish absorption and more consistent color (page 127). For a fine finish, some woods are best treated with grain filler instead of sealer (page 129).

The next layer is the color layer, which is usually created with wood stain or penetrating oil (pages 132 to 137). Color can either enhance or minimize grain pattern and other wood features, and it can beautify plain wood. With fine woods, or to create a more rustic look, the color layer can be omitted. Dampen the wood surface with mineral spirits to see how it will look with a clear finish. To create a specific decorative look, or to cover wood defects, apply paint as the color layer (pages 138 to 143).

Finally, a topcoat is applied to seal the wood and protect the finished surface from scratches and wear. Topcoats can be created with traditional finishing products, like tung oil, or more contemporary materials, like polyurethane (pages 144 to 153). A layer or two of well-buffed paste wax can be applied over most topcoat materials to create a glossy, protective surface that is easily renewable with fresh wax.

When selecting a finish, it helps if you know the wood species of your project. Softwoods, like pine, should always be treated with sanding sealer or primer, for example. And open-grained hardwoods, like red oak or mahogany, look better when treated with grain filler.

As a general rule, base your finish selection on color. Simply choose a color you like, then select a coloring agent and a compatible topcoat.

Consider use, as well. If the finished piece will be used by children or as a food preparation surface, use nontoxic water-based products to finish the wood. For more information on finishing products, refer to the sections indicated above.

A typical wood finish is composed of three basic layers: the seal coat, the color layer, and the topcoat.

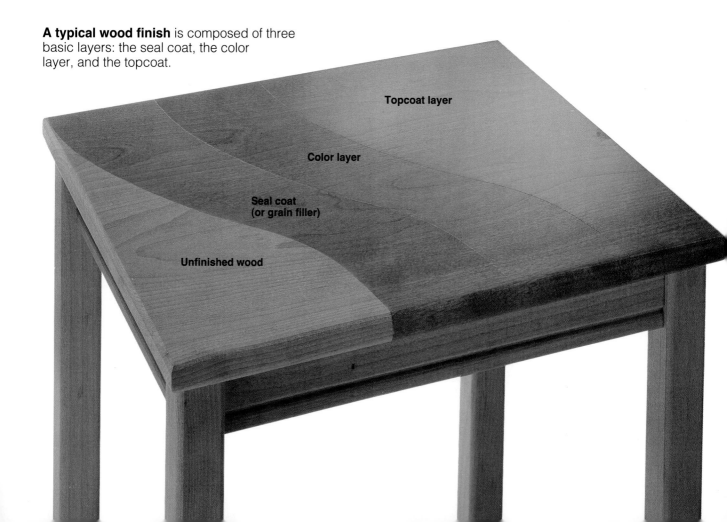

Topcoat layer

Color layer

Seal coat (or grain filler)

Unfinished wood

Tips for Selecting a New Finish

Consider absorption rates. Some wood types absorb more finish materials than others, depending on the porosity of the wood grain. In the photo above, the same stain was applied to three different unsealed woods, resulting in three very different levels of darkness. Sealing the wood with sanding sealer or filling the grain minimizes this effect.

Consider the grain pattern when choosing a finish. Highly figured wood, like the walnut shown above, usually is given a clear finish so the grain is not obscured. In some cases, however, tinted penetrating oil can be used to enhance an already striking grain pattern. Experiment with different coloring agents on a piece of similar wood, or in an inconspicuous area of the project, to help with the finish selection.

Look for repairs, damage, and uneven color. Workpieces with obvious damage or repairs, like the wood putty line shown above, or with uneven wood color from old finish residue, require a darker finish to disguise the wood defects.

Consider combining colors to create interesting decorative effects. Contrasting stains on the same wood type can create a dramatic finish when used with good design sense.

Sand wood with power sanders, like the random-orbit sander shown above, to make quick work of the initial finish sanding stages, while producing a very smooth wood surface.

Preparing the Wood Surface

A properly prepared wood surface absorbs finish materials evenly, focusing attention on the quality and color of the wood and the finish. A poorly prepared surface focuses attention on itself and its flaws.

Sanding or filling scratches and gouges, removing dents and stains, and carefully finish sanding are the essential steps in preparing for the finish on any home built-in, woodworking, or refinishing project. With many woods (especially softwoods like pine) you can create a more even finish by sealing the wood with sanding sealer immediately after finish sanding, then sanding the sealer lightly with 220-grit sandpaper after it dries. For exceptionally smooth, rich finishes (particularly on open-grain hardwoods like mahogany), apply wood grain filler to fill in checks and large pores, creating a smooth-as-glass surface.

Before beginning the final preparations for the finish, sand the workpiece with medium-grit sandpaper to remove small scratches and other surface problems. Any scratches, gouges, dents, or stains that survive the intermediate sanding should be remedied before you finish-sand.

Do your final stage of finish sanding immediately before you apply the finish—the smooth surface created by finish sanding is easily scratched or discolored.

This section shows:

• Making Final Surface Preparations
  (pages 128 to 129)

Tips for Preparing a Wood Surface

Sandpaper Grit Chart

Grit	Task
80 to 100	Finish removal
120 to150	Preliminary finish sanding
180	Final sanding for softwood; intermediate stage of finish sanding for hardwood
220	Final sanding for hardwood
300 to 400	Sanding between finish layers
600 wet/dry	Wet sanding of final finish layer

Nonstainable wood putty   **Stainable wood putty**

Choose the right sandpaper for the job. *Aluminum oxide* and *garnet* are two common types. Aluminum oxide is a good general-use product suitable for most refinishing and finishing purposes. Garnet is usually cheaper than aluminum oxide, but it wears out much more quickly. Use sandpaper with the proper grit (higher numbers indicate finer grit—see chart above).

Use stainable wood putty to repair scratches and gouges in unfinished wood. Finish materials are not absorbed by nonstainable wood putty, which is usually meant to be used for touch-up after the finish is applied. Read container labels carefully before you purchase wood putty.

Apply wood grain filler that approximately matches the natural color of your wood. Available in light and dark colors, grain filler creates a smooth surface in open wood grains. Usually manufactured as a gel, it can be applied with a putty knife or a rag, but the excess material should be wiped off with a plastic scraper (page 129).

Make your own sanding sealer by blending one part clear topcoat material with one part topcoat solvent. NOTE: Use the same topcoat material you plan to apply to the project. Sanding sealer is used before coloring soft or open-grain woods to achieve even stain penetration. To apply, wipe on a heavy coat, then wipe off the excess after a few minutes. Sand lightly with 220-grit sandpaper when dry.

With grain filler

With sanding sealer

Finish-sanded only

Making Final Surface Preparations

Ensure an even, quality finish by carefully preparing the wood surface. Finish-sand with progressively finer grits of sandpaper, starting with 150-grit. Generally, hardwood requires finer-grit sandpaper than softwood (see chart on page 127). For speed and even results, use a power sander for the first stages of finish sanding. Use hand-sanding with the finest grit in the sequence so you do not oversand.

Seal wood with sanding sealer to create more even finish absorption. Apply grain filler to open-grain hardwood for a deep, smooth finish. Because they decrease stain absorption, sealing and filling create lighter finishes.

Use sanding sealer or grain filler for a fine finish. Finish sanding alone creates a smooth surface, but because wood absorbs stain at different rates, the color can be blotchy and dark. Sealing with sanding sealer (page 127) evens out the stain-absorption rates, yielding a lighter, more even finish. Filling the grain creates a lighter finish that feels as smooth as it looks.

Everything You Need:

Tools: finishing sander, sanding blocks, plastic scraper, work light, wire brush.

Materials: sandpaper, abrasive pads, cloths, sanding sealer or grain filler.

Tips for Finish Sanding

Examine the workpiece with bright sidelighting during finish sanding to gauge your progress. If shadows, scratches, or sanding marks are visible, more sanding is needed.

Wipe the wood surface clean whenever you change sandpaper grits, using a cloth slightly dampened with mineral spirits. This removes dust and grit from coarser sandpaper that cause scratches when you continue sanding.

Clean your sandpaper regularly with a wire brush to remove sawdust and grit that can clog the sandpaper and cause burnishing of the wood surface.

How to Finish-sand

1 Finish-sand all surfaces with 150-grit sandpaper, following the direction of the grain. Use a finishing sander on flat surfaces and specialty sanding blocks on contours. When sanding hardwood, switch to 180-grit paper and sand again (see chart, page 127).

2 Raise the wood grain by dampening the surface with a wet rag. Let the wood dry, then skim the surface with a fine abrasive pad, following the grain. The pad pulls out raised fibers, decreasing the chance of raising the grain during finishing.

3 Use sanding blocks to hand-sand the entire workpiece with the finest-grit paper in the sanding sequence. Sand until all sanding marks are gone and the surface is smooth. If using sanding sealer (page 127), apply a coat now, then sand lightly with 220-grit when dry.

How to Apply Grain Filler

1 After finish sanding, use a rag or putty knife to spread a coat of grain filler (page 127) onto the wood surface. With a polishing motion, work the filler into the grain. Let the filler dry until it becomes cloudy (usually about five minutes).

2 Remove excess filler by drawing a plastic putty scraper across the grain of the wood at a 45° angle. Let the grain filler dry overnight.

3 Lightly hand-sand the surface, following the direction of the grain, with 320-grit sandpaper. Clean thoroughly with a cloth dampened in mineral spirits before applying the finish.

129

Preparation Tips

Fill nail holes and gaps in wood surfaces, using untinted wood filler. Let the filler dry completely before sanding the surfaces. On plywood surfaces that will be painted, fill any void areas along exposed edges.

Sand hardwood face frames to smooth the joints and remove surface defects. first, sand with a belt sander and 80-grit sanding belt (left), using light pressure to avoid gouging the wood. Then sand with a pad sander and 120-grit sandpaper (right). Change to 220-grit sandpaper for the final sanding. Always move the sander in the same direction as the wood grain, and replace sanding sheets as they become worn.

Sand edged plywood shelves carefully. To avoid sanding through the surface veneer, make light pencil marks on the plywood surface next to the hardwood edging, then sand across the top of the edging just until the pencil marks are removed.

Use a hand sanding block and 220-grit sandpaper to sand corners and other areas where the pad sander will not fit.

Clean all sanded surfaces with a brush and vacuum, then wipe them with a tack cloth.

Finishing Tips

Protect walls from stains by sliding a sheet of wax paper or plastic between the trim moldings and the wall before applying oil finish or paint.

Scrape away dried glue before painting or finishing, using an old chisel with the corners rounded off. Finishing oils and paint will not penetrate glue, so any excess must be removed completely before finish is applied.

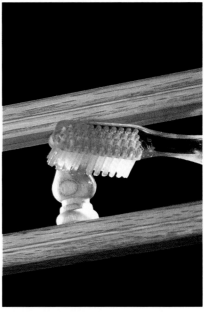

Use a toothbrush to apply finishes to hard-to-reach areas, like spindle-and-rail moldings and other ornamental trim pieces.

Protect surfaces that will be glued, if you are finishing the pieces before assembling the built-in. Glue will not bond to oiled or stained wood, so cover joint areas with masking tape before applying finishing materials.

Use a tinted filler stick to fill nail holes in finished wood. Filler sticks come in many tones, but if none matches the finish of your built-in exactly, blend putty from different sticks to create the color you need.

Use heat-activated veneer tape to cover unfinished edges of plywood or particleboard panels on built-ins without face frames. Bond the tape with a household iron, then rub the tape with a block of hardwood. Trim the overhang with a utility knife, then lightly sand the edges to smooth them.

A well-chosen, properly applied color layer is the most important component of an attractive wood finish.

Coloring Wood

There are several reasons to color wood. The most common reason is to enhance the appearance of wood by showing off a fine or distinctive grain pattern or creating a beautiful wood tone. But stain and penetrating oil, the two most basic coloring agents, can accomplish more practical results as well. Using a dark color conceals uneven color in your wood and can blend together two or more different wood types—a common problem encountered in refinishing.

When selecting a coloring agent for your project, you will find a vast selection of products to choose from. There are oil-based stains, water-based stains, wipe-on gel stains, penetrating oils, one-step stain-and-sealant products...the options seem endless. To sort through the many products and make the selection that is best for your project, start by finding a color you like. Then check the specific properties of the coloring agent to determine if it is the best general

type for your project. Make sure it has no compatibility problems with the topcoat you plan to use, or with any old finish materials that have not been removed (see charts, next page).

Whichever coloring agent you select, read the directions very carefully before applying it to the wood. Drying time, application techniques, and cleanup methods vary widely between products—even products that are similar. Also test the product on a wood sample similar to your project. When using a stain, apply enough coats to create the exact color shade you want (stain will become darker with each new coat that is applied). Keep a careful record of how many coats you applied for your reference when you finish the actual workpiece.

This section shows:

- Coloring with Penetrating Oil (page 135)
- Coloring with Stain (pages 136 to 137)

Penetrating Oil

Penetrating oil (often called "Danish oil" or "rubbing oil") delivers color deep into the wood for a rich-looking finish that can be buffed to form a protective surface.

Advantages:
- easy to apply
- creates very even coloration
- does not "paint over" wood grain
- compatible with most topcoats
- penetrates deeper than stain for very rich color
- can be used without a topcoat

Drawbacks:
- may fade in direct sunlight
- limited range of colors
- cannot darken color with multiple coats
- toxic fumes; flammable

Compatibility:
- avoid using with oil-based polyurethane

Recommended Uses:
- wood with attractive grain pattern
- antiques and fine furniture
- decorative items

Common Brand Names:
- Watco® Danish Oil Finish, Deft® Danish Oil Finish

Water-based Liquid Stain

Water-based liquid stain is wiped or brushed onto the wood surface to create a color layer that can be darkened with additional applications.

Advantages:
- easy to clean up, safe to use
- wide range of colors available
- can be built up in layers to control final color
- dries quickly

Drawbacks:
- can raise wood grain (requires sanding for an even surface)
- can chip or scuff if not properly topcoated

Compatibility:
- bonds well with most topcoats

Recommended Uses:
- floors
- woodwork
- previously finished furniture—can be "painted" on to cover color variations
- tabletops, eating surfaces, children's furniture and toys

Common Brand Names:
- Carver Tripp® Safe & Simple Wood Stain, Behr® Water-based Stain, Varathane Elite Wood Stain®

Oil-based Liquid Stain

Oil-based liquid traditionally has been the most common type of wood stain, but its availability and popularity are declining due to environmental factors.

Advantages:
- does not raise wood grain
- slow drying time increases workability
- permanent and colorfast
- can be built up to control color
- conditions and seals wood
- less likely to bleed than water-based stain

Drawbacks:
- harmful vapors; flammable; hard to clean
- regulated or restricted in some states
- decreasing availability
- unpleasant odor

Compatibility:
- can be used with most topcoats

Recommended Uses:
- previously stained wood
- wood finish touch-up

Common Brand Names:
- Minwax® Wood Finish, Carver Tripp® Wood Stain, Zar® Wood Stain

Gel Stain

Gel stains, usually oil-based, provide even surface color that is highly controllable due to the thickness of the product. Gel finishes are growing in popularity.

Advantages:
- very neat and easy to apply—will not run
- does not raise wood grain
- dries evenly
- can be built up to deepen color
- can be buffed to create a hard surface

Drawbacks:
- limited color selection
- more expensive than other stain types
- hard to clean up
- requires buffing between coats

Compatibility:
- can be used with most topcoats

Recommended Uses:
- woodwork and furniture with vertical surfaces
- furniture with spindles and other rounded parts

Common Brand Names:
- Bartley® Gel Stain, Behlen® Master Gel

Tips for Coloring Wood

Mask the staining area to help prevent stain from bleeding into adjacent areas. As an added precaution, lightly score along the borders of the staining area with a craft knife to cut the wood fibers so they cannot draw the coloring agent out of the staining area. Applying wood sealer (page 127) also makes it easier to keep wood coloring agents from bleeding.

Even out color by using dark stain, like the red mahogany stain being applied to this stripped door. Some wood is discolored after stripping, and using a darker stain is an easy alternative to spending hours or even days sanding the wood to completely remove all of the stain. Because it forms a more opaque color layer, wood stain is generally a better product than penetrating oil for covering wood problems.

Test coloring agents on an inconspicuous area of the workpiece to see how the color will look once the stain is applied and dry. Coloring agents often have a very different appearance on the actual workpiece than on color chips at the store display.

Seal exposed end grain with sanding sealer, then sand lightly with 220-grit sandpaper. Unsealed end grain absorbs more stain than face grain, causing it to look darker. Be careful to keep sealer off the face-grain areas.

Use a clean, lint-free cloth when wiping penetrating oil or stain onto wood surfaces. Rags from well-worn cotton T-shirts make excellent staining cloths.

Coloring with Penetrating Oil

Penetrating oil is an excellent product for creating even, natural wood tones that do not obscure the wood grain. Often called Danish oil or rubbing oil, most penetrating oil is fortified with tung oil or other hardening agents that allow it to be buffed to a hard surface after application. When applied to decorative items and furniture that does not receive a significant amount of wear, penetrating oil can be used without a topcoat for a deep, low-luster finish.

When using penetrating oil, be sure to follow the manufacturer's recommendations for application and drying time. In some woods, oil finishes will seep out of wood pores for up to 72 hours while the finish dries.

Everything You Need:

Materials: staining cloths, tinted penetrating oil, fine abrasive pads.

Apply penetrating oil in heavy coats, using a clean staining rag.

How to Color Wood with Penetrating Oil

1 Prepare for the stain (page 134), then apply a heavy coat of penetrating oil to all surfaces, using a staining cloth. Wait 15 to 30 minutes, recoating any areas that begin to dry out. Apply oil to all surfaces, and let it soak into the wood for 30 to 60 minutes.

2 Wipe the surface dry with a clean cloth, rubbing with the wood grain. Apply another coat of oil with a clean cloth, then let the oil dry overnight. NOTE: Two coats are sufficient in most cases, since further coats will not darken the finish color.

3 Dab a few drops of penetrating oil onto a fine abrasive pad, then rub the surfaces until smooth. Let the oil dry for at least 72 hours before applying a topcoat. If you do not plan to topcoat the finish, buff with a soft cloth to harden the oil finish.

Coloring with Stain

"Wood stain" is a general term describing a number of different coloring agents with very different properties (page 133).

Oil-based or water-based, in liquid form or as a gel, stain is a very controllable coloring agent. The color often can be lightened by scrubbing, and it usually can be darkened by applying additional coats.

Before staining, seal all end grain and test the stain color (page 134).

Everything You Need:

Tools: paint brushes.

Materials: sanding sealer, staining cloths, liquid or gel stain, fine abrasive pads, sandpaper.

Creating consistent color is easy with stain, especially gel stain (above), which clings to awkward surfaces without pooling.

How to Apply Liquid Stain

1 Prepare for the stain (page 134), then stir the stain thoroughly and apply a heavy coat with a brush or cloth. Stir the stain often as you work. Let the stain soak in for about 15 minutes (see manufacturer's directions).

2 Remove excess stain with a clean, lint-free cloth. Wipe against the grain first, then with the grain. If the color is too dark, try scrubbing with water or mineral spirits. Let the stain dry, then buff with a fine abrasive pad.

3 Apply light coats of stain until the desired color tone is achieved, buffing with an abrasive pad between coats. Buff the final coat of stain before top-coating.

How to Apply Gel Stain

1 Prepare for the stain (page 134). Stir the gel stain, then work it into the surfaces of the workpiece with a staining cloth, using a circular motion. Cover as much of the workpiece as you can reach with the staining cloth, recoating any areas that dry out as you work. Gel stain penetrates better if it is worked into the wood with a brush or rag, rather than simply wiped onto the wood surface.

2 Use a stiff-bristled brush, like this stenciling brush, to apply gel stain into hard-to-reach areas, where it is difficult to use a staining cloth.

3 Let the stain soak in (see manufacturer's directions), then wipe off the excess with a clean rag, using a polishing motion. Buff the stained surface with the wood grain, using a soft, clean cloth.

4 Apply additional coats of stain until the workpiece has reached the desired color tone. Gel stain manufacturers usually recommend at least three coats to provide a thick stain layer that helps protect the wood against scratches and other surface flaws. Let the stain dry, then buff with a fine abrasive pad before applying a topcoat.

Painting Wood

Use paint as an alternative to wood stain to give plain wood a splash of color or a decorative touch; or simply use it to hide wear, low-quality materials, or unattractive wood.

Furniture and woodwork generally should be painted with water-based or oil-based enamel paint—except when using a few decorative painting techniques that call for flat wall paint (pages 142 to 143). Enamel paint forms a tough, protective coat that resists moisture, chipping, and scratching. It is available in dozens of premixed colors, and in gloss and semi-gloss versions. Or, you can have special colors custom-mixed at a paint store.

This section shows:

- Applying Paint (pages 140 to 141)
- Decorative Painting (pages 142 to 143)

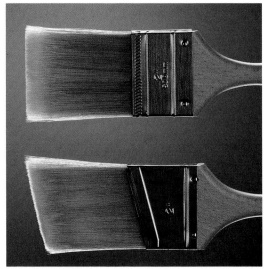

Paint brushes for wood include straight trim brushes for flat areas, and tapered brushes for edges. Use synthetic brushes (nylon or polyester bristles) for both water-based and oil-based paint.

Water-based Paint

Water-based paint for wood is usually sold as "latex enamel" or "acrylic enamel." Because water-based paint can raise wood grain, use a water-based primer to prepare the wood, then sand the primed surface before applying the paint. The coloring agents in water-based paint settle quickly, so stir the paint often as you work.

Advantages:
- safer for the environment
- less toxic than oil-based paints
- easy cleanup with soap and water
- dries quickly
- can be thinned with water

Drawbacks:
- raises wood grain
- scratches easily
- cleanup is difficult after paint dries
- softens with exposure to moisture
- cannot be applied in thick coats

Compatibility:
- will not adhere to most topcoats
- may be used over other water-based paints

Recommended Uses:
- children's toys and furniture
- cabinetry
- woodwork

Oil-based Paint

Oil-based paint (also called alkyd paint) dries to a harder finish than water-based paint and offers the best protection for wood that is exposed to wear. It is still the preferred paint type of most professional painters, but this preference is changing as water-based paints become stronger and more versatile. Use oil-based primer with oil-based paint.

Advantages:
- hard, scratch-resistant finish
- unaffected by moisture
- does not raise wood grain
- dries to a very smooth finish

Drawbacks:
- releases toxic vapors
- slow drying time
- requires mineral spirits for cleanup
- use is restricted in some states

Compatibility:
- may be applied over varnish or oil-based polyurethane
- may be used over oil- or water-based paints

Recommended Uses:
- stairs and railings
- floors and doors
- woodwork
- previously finished wood

Painting Tips

Stir paint with a mixing bit attached to a portable drill for fast, thorough mixing. Keep the mixer bit moving constantly. Repeatedly lower the mixer blade to the bottom of the can, then raise it to the top of the can to mix in settled pigment.

Strain paint to remove lumps, dirt, and other foreign materials from paint. Commercial paint strainers are available, or you can make your own from cheese-cloth or nylon stockings.

Applying Paint

Painting wood is very much like painting walls and other common do-it-yourself painting projects. Whenever you paint anything, preparation is critical. For wood, that means sanding the surface until it is flat and smooth, then sealing with primer so the paint absorbs evenly (see *Tips,* below). Although it is a different product, primer is applied using the same techniques as paint. In addition to sealing the wood, it keeps resins in the wood from bleeding through the paint layer.

Cleanup solvents, thinning agents, drying time, and coverage vary widely from one enamel paint to another. Read the manufacturer's directions carefully. For best results, designate a clean, dust-free area for painting (pages 154 to 157).

For a smooth surface free from lap marks, hold your paint brush at a 45° angle, and apply just enough pressure to flex the bristles slightly.

Everything You Need:

Tools: paint brushes, sanding block.

Materials: primer, paint, clean rags, tack cloth, sandpaper, masking tape, polyurethane.

Tips for Preparing Wood for Painting

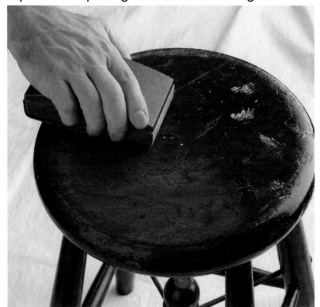

Previously painted wood can be repainted without priming, but if the old painted surface is badly chipped or damaged, primer is helpful. Fill scratches and nicks with wood putty (pages 127 to 129), and sand the surface smooth before painting.

Clear finished wood should be stripped and sanded before priming. Paint will not adhere well to most topcoat finishes.

How to Paint Wood

1 Finish-sand the wood (pages 128 to 129). Vacuum the surfaces or wipe with a tack cloth after you sand to remove all traces of sanding dust from the workpiece.

2 Prime the wood with an even coat of primer (use water-based primer with water-based paint, and oil-based primer with oil-based paint). Smooth out brush marks as you work, and sand with 220-grit sandpaper when dry.

3 Mask any adjacent areas that will be painted a different color, using masking tape. Press the edges of the tape firmly against the wood.

4 Apply a thin coat of paint, brushing with the grain. When dry, sand with 400-grit sandpaper, then wipe with a tack cloth. Apply at least one more heavier coat, sanding and wiping with a tack cloth between additional coats. Do not sand the last coat.

OPTION: Apply clear polyurethane topcoat to surfaces that will get heavy wear. Before applying, wet-sand the paint with 600-grit wet/dry sandpaper, then wipe with a tack cloth. Use water-based polyurethane over latex paint, and oil-based over oil-based paint.

Decorative Painting

Apply a creative touch to your project with decorative painting techniques. Farmhouse finishes, stencil finishes, and color washes are techniques that give furniture and decorative items a rustic, Early American look. A handful of specialty paint brushes, some quality finishing materials, a few helpful tools, like stencils, and a little creativity are all you need to create these unique painted finishes on your project.

Farmhouse finishes re-create the look of worn paint. Apply a base coat of wood stain, followed by a top-coat of shellac. Paint a layer of water-based paint over the dried shellac. Once the paint is dry, sand off randomly chosen areas of paint with 100-grit sandpaper, applying varying degrees of pressure to imitate natural wear. Sand the corners of the workpiece and any detail areas with 220-grit sandpaper, then wipe with a lint-free cloth and denatured alcohol to complete the farmhouse finish.

Stenciled designs add a bright, decorative touch to topcoated or painted wood. Purchase clear acetate stencils at a craft store (or cut your own). Position the stencil on the wood, and secure it with tape. Stipple the wood by dabbing paint (acrylic craft paints are a good choice for stenciling) onto the surface through the stencil, using a stenciling brush. Allow the paint to dry before removing the stencil. If more than one color will be used, realign the stencil and apply each color, one at a time (start with the lightest color).

Color washes produce a thin, semi-transparent coat of paint on bare wood. Dilute water-based paint by mixing one part paint to four parts water (the more diluted the paint mixture, the thinner the paint layer will be). Brush the thinned paint onto the wood, working with the grain. Wipe the surface immediately with a lint-free cloth, removing paint until you achieve the desired color tone. Repeat the process to darken the color, if needed. Soften the look by scuffing the painted surface with a fine abrasive pad when dry.

Protect your finish and wood with a topcoat layer, like the wipe-on tung oil being applied to this dresser.

Applying Topcoats

Topcoat finishes seal the wood, protect the finish from scratches and other wear, and increase the visual appeal of the wood. Because they dry clear, topcoats highlight the coloring and natural figure of the wood. For most projects, a topcoat of tung oil finish, polyurethane, or paste wax will give your wood the protection it needs and the finished appearance you desire.

When choosing a topcoat, consider durability, sheen, and compatibility with any coloring layers you use (see opposite page). Other factors, like drying time, ease of application and cleanup, and safeness, should also influence your choice. If possible, check samples at building centers or paint stores to see if a particular topcoat is suitable for your workpiece.

Some one-step stain-and-seal products are also available. Test these products on scrap wood before using them on good furniture.

This section shows:

• Applying Tung Oil Finishes (page 147)
• Applying Polyurethane (pages 148 to 151)
• Applying Wax (pages 152 to 153)

Make tack cloths by moistening cheesecloth in mineral spirits. Apply a spoonful of varnish (or any other clear topcoat material) to the cheesecloth, and knead the cloth until the varnish is absorbed evenly. Make several tack cloths and store them in a glass jar with a lid.

144

Tung Oil Finish

Tung oil is a natural oil drawn from the nut of the tung tree. Good for creating a matte or glossy hand-rubbed finish, tung oil products are available in clear and tinted form.

Advantages:
- easy to apply
- flexible finish that resists cracking
- very natural appearance that makes minimal changes in wood appearance
- penetrates into the wood
- easily renewed and repaired

Drawbacks:
- not as durable as other topcoats

Compatibility:
- not compatible with polyurethane

Recommended Uses:
- uneven surfaces like chairs and other furniture with spindles
- woodwork
- antiques
- wood with highly figured grain

Common Brand Names:
- Minwax® Tung Oil Finish, Zar® Tung Oil, Tung Seal by McCloskey®

Water-based Polyurethane

Water-based polyurethane is an increasingly popular topcoat because of its fast drying time and easy clean-up. Its hazard-free disposal and low toxicity are a plus.

Advantages:
- fast drying time
- easy cleanup
- nonflammable
- nontoxic
- impervious to water and alcohol

Drawbacks:
- can raise wood grain
- can have an unnatural "plastic" appearance

Compatibility:
- do not apply over other topcoats, or directly over commercial sanding sealer

Recommended Uses:
- floors
- interior woodwork and furniture
- children's furniture and toys
- tabletops, eating surfaces

Common Brand Names:
- EnviroCare®, Varathane® Diamond Finish, Carver Tripp® Safe & Simple, Zar® Polyurethane

Oil-based Polyurethane

Traditionally, polyurethane has been an oil-based product. Despite the emergence of water-based polyurethanes, many refinishers still prefer this more familiar product.

Advantages:
- easier to get a smooth finish than with a water-based polyurethane
- forms durable, hard finish
- impervious to water and alcohol

Drawbacks:
- slow drying time
- disposal and use closely regulated in some states
- decreasing availability
- difficult cleanup
- toxic
- gives off smelly fumes

Compatibility:
- not compatible with other topcoats

Recommended Uses:
- furniture
- surfaces where a very thick, durable topcoat is desired

Common Brand Names:
- Defthane by Deft®, Heirloom Varnish by McCloskey®, Minwax® Polyurethane

Paste Wax

Paste wax is a blend of natural waxes, dissolved with mineral spirits or naphtha. It is favored for its hand-rubbed sheen and natural appearance.

Advantages:
- easy to renew with fresh coats
- very natural appearance
- can be buffed to desired sheen
- can be applied over most topcoats

Drawbacks:
- easily scratched and worn away
- needs to be restored regularly
- water or alcohol spills will damage wax

Compatibility:
- no restrictions

Recommended Uses:
- antiques
- fine furniture
- floors

Common Brand Names:
- Antiquax®, Johnson & Johnson® Paste Wax, Minwax® Paste Finishing Wax

Tips for Applying Topcoats

Stir topcoat finishes gently with a clean stir stick. Shaking the container or stirring too vigorously can create air bubbles that cause pockmarks in the finish when dry.

Transfer leftover topcoat materials to smaller containers to minimize the amount of air that can react with the product. Tung oil and polyurethane are especially susceptible to thickening when exposed to air.

Sand between topcoat layers, using 600-grit wet/dry sandpaper, to smooth out the finish. Wipe down the worksurface with a tack cloth after sanding. Save time and ensure better results by creating a clean, dust-free work area (pages 154 to 157). NOTE: See product label; topcoat requirements will vary.

Wet-sand with a fine abrasive pad on the final topcoat layer to create a finish with the exact amount of gloss you want.

Applying Tung Oil Finishes

Tung oil is an extremely popular finish, both for its easy application and its appearance. Several well-buffed coats applied with a clean cloth will form a suitably hard finish. With added coats and more buffing, you can achieve a glossy finish. Tung-oil-based products are suitable for most furniture, including antiques. Seldom sold in pure form, tung oil is usually blended with tinting agents or other topcoats, and is usually described by manufacturers as "tung oil finish."

Because tung oil forms a relatively thin coat, renew finished surfaces with a fresh coat of tung oil every year or so. Or, you can apply a protective layer of paste wax to guard the finish, and renew the wax topcoat periodically. Use lemon oil to refresh a tung oil finish without recoating.

Everything You Need:

Tools: assorted paint brushes.

Materials: clean cloth, rubber gloves, mineral spirits, tung oil finish, abrasive pads.

Use a paint brush to apply tung oil to very uneven surfaces. Because the excess tung oil is wiped off before it dries, there is no need to worry about lap marks from brushes.

How to Apply Tung Oil Finish

1 Clean the surfaces thoroughly with a cloth and mineral spirits. Apply a thick coat of tung oil finish with a cloth or brush. Let the tung oil penetrate for 5 to 10 minutes, then rub off the excess with a cloth, using a polishing motion.

2 Buff the tung oil with a clean cloth after 24 hours, then reapply additional coats, as needed, to build the desired finish—three coats is generally considered the minimum for a good finish. Use a clean cloth for each application.

3 Let the finish dry completely, then buff it lightly with a fine abrasive pad. For a higher gloss, buff with a polishing bonnet and portable drill.

Applying Polyurethane

Polyurethane (often called polyurethane varnish or simply varnish) is a hard, durable topcoat material commonly used on floors, countertops, and other heavy-use surfaces. Available in both water-based and oil-based form (page 145), polyurethane is a complex mixture of plastic resins, solvents, and drying oils or water, that dries to a clear, nonyellowing finish.

A wide array of finishing products contain some type of polyurethane, which can cause a good deal of confusion. If a label uses the descriptive terms "acrylic" or "polymerized," the product is most likely polyurethane-based. Your safest bet in choosing the best polyurethane product for the job is to refer to the suggestions for use on the product label.

Everything You Need

Tools: vacuum cleaner, painting pad with pole extension, paint brushes.

Materials: polyurethane, mineral spirits, medium and fine abrasive pads, felt pad, staining cloths.

For safe use and low toxicity, water-based polyurethane is an excellent choice. Use it for children's furniture and toys, as well as for eating surfaces.

Tips for Choosing Polyurethane Products

Choose the finish gloss that best meets your needs. Product availability has expanded among polyurethane products in recent years to include gloss, semi-gloss, and matte (or satin) sheens. Because of the expanding product lines, polyurethane-based topcoat products have almost completely replaced traditional wood varnish.

Hardening agents are available for some brands of water-based polyurethane for outdoor applications or high-traffic areas. Hardening agents lose their effectiveness quickly, so harden only as much product as you plan to apply in one coat.

Tips for Using Polyurethane

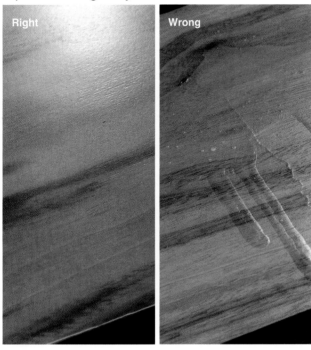

Apply polyurethane in several thin layers (left) for best results. Applying too much finish at once (right) slows down the drying time, and causes running, wrinkling, or sagging.

Brush out lap marks to create a smooth surface before the polyurethane dries. Small brush marks will show, but will blend together as the finish dries. Because it dries slowly, oil-based polyurethane gives you more time to brush out lap marks.

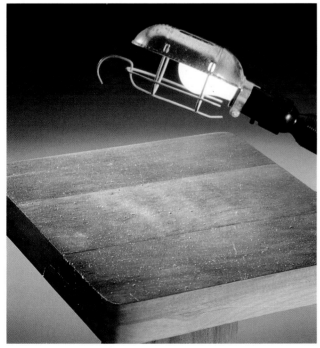

Examine the surface after each coat of polyurethane dries, using a bright side light. Wet-sand with a fine abrasive pad to remove dust and other surface problems, like air bubbles. After sanding, wipe the surface clean with a tack cloth.

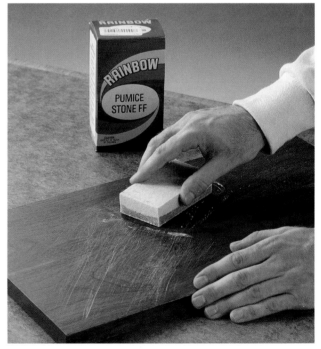

Wet-sand with fine pumice powder as a maintenance technique for removing scratches and scuffs in a hardened polyurethane finish. Sprinkle the pumice powder over the surface flaw, then rub with a felt pad or a cloth dipped in mineral spirits.

How to Apply Polyurethane to Furniture

1 Seal unstained wood with a 1:1 mixture of polyurethane and thinning agent (check product label), applied with a clean cloth or brush. Let the sealer dry. Wipe off excess sealer with a clean cloth. NOTE: Furniture that has been colored with stain or penetrating oil does not need a seal-coat.

2 Apply a coat of polyurethane, starting at the top of the project and working your way down. Use a good-quality brush. When the surface is covered, smooth out the finish by lightly brushing in one direction only, parallel to the grain. Let dry, then sand between coats, using 600-grit wet/dry sandpaper.

3 Apply the second coat. To keep the finish from running, always try to position the workpiece so the surface being topcoated is horizontal.

4 OPTION: After the final coat dries, wet-sand the surface with a fine abrasive pad to remove any small imperfections and diminish the gloss.

How to Apply Polyurethane to Floors

1 Seal sanded wood with a 1:1 mixture of water-based polyurethane and water, applied with a painting pad and pole extension. Let the seal coat dry, then use a medium abrasive pad to lightly buff the surfaces to remove any raised wood grain caused by the water. Vacuum the surface with a bristle attachment, or wipe with a tack cloth.

2 Apply a coat of undiluted polyurethane to the floor. Apply the finish as evenly as possible. Do not overbrush.

3 Let the finish dry, then buff the floor with a medium abrasive pad. Vacuum or wipe the floor. Apply more coats of polyurethane as needed to build the finish to the desired thickness, buffing between coats. Most floors require at least three coats of water-based polyurethane for a hard, durable finish (see manufacturer's recommendations).

4 **OPTION:** When the final coat of finish is dry, buff the surfaces with water and a fine abrasive pad to remove surface imperfections and diminish the gloss.

Applying Wax

Wax is an easily renewable topcoat that protects and beautifies wood. It is often applied over oil finishes and other topcoats to absorb small scratches and everyday wear and tear. Then, simply by removing the old wax and applying a fresh coat, you can create a new-looking topcoat without refinishing.

Paste wax is the best wax product for wood because it can be buffed to a hard finish. But other types of wax, like liquid wax, can be used for specific purposes.

Apply several coats of paste wax for best results. The hardness of a wax finish is a direct result of the thickness of the wax and the vigor with which it is buffed. Extensive buffing also increases the glossiness of the finish.

For the hardest possible finish, choose products with a high ratio of wax to solvent (see label).

Everything You Need:

Tools: fine abrasive pads.

Materials: paste wax, clean cloth.

Tips for Applying Wax to Furniture

Use liquid wax on detailed areas, where paste wax is difficult to apply. Apply the wax with a stiff brush, then buff with a soft cloth.

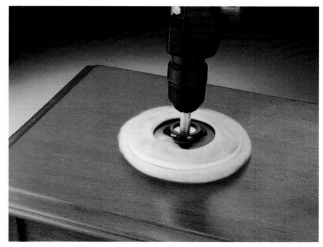

Buff wax to a hard, glossy finish with a polishing bonnet attached to a portable drill. Keep the drill moving to avoid overheating the wax.

How to Apply Paste Wax

1 Apply a moderate layer of paste wax to the wood using a fine abrasive pad or a cloth. Rub the wax into the wood with a polishing motion.

2 Allow the wax to dry until it becomes filmy in spots (above). Gently wipe off any excess, undried wax, then allow the entire wax surface to dry until filmy (usually within 10 to 20 minutes). NOTE: Do not let the wax dry too long, or it will harden and become very difficult to buff.

3 Begin buffing the wax with a soft cloth, using a light, circular motion. Buff the entire surface until the filminess disappears and the wax is clear.

4 Continue buffing the wax until the surface is hard and shiny. Apply and buff another coat, then let the wax dry for at least 24 hours before applying additional coats. Apply at least three coats for a fine wax finish.

Safety, Cleanup & Disposal

Install fans in windows in your work area to provide ventilation. Where possible, direct one fan outside to remove vapors, and direct another fan into the room to supply fresh air.

Protect yourself and your home, and help ensure good finishing results by using sensible safety, cleanup, and disposal methods when finishing.

Finishing wood can create many hazards, including dangerous vapors, flammable or toxic chemical residue, and sanding dust that can impair breathing (as well as ruin an otherwise good finish).

Make sure you have the required safety and protective equipment before you begin working (next page). Establish a dedicated work area, preferably in a well-ventilated area, like a garage. Organize the area for comfort, safety, and efficiency (see guidelines, left). If you are unsure about any disposal regulations, contact your local waste management department, city office, or the Environmental Protection Agency (page 156).

Guidelines for a Finishing Work Area

- Choose a worksurface that raises the project to a comfortable working height. An adjustable-height workbench is ideal for finishing.
- Store knives, scrapers, and other dangerous tools in a locked cabinet or trunk.
- Store hazardous or flammable materials in a fireproof cabinet.
- Protect the floor with a drop cloth. For messy jobs, lay old newspaper over the drop cloth for easy cleanup.
- Cover any ductwork in the work area to keep dust and fumes from spreading throughout the house.
- Extinguish nearby pilot lights and do not operate space heaters whenever working with strippers and other chemicals that produce flammable vapors.
- Maintain a work area that is well lit, dry, and warm (between 65° and 75°F). Use a dehumidifier in damp areas to speed drying times.
- Use a metal trash can with a lid and empty it regularly.

Read product labels for important information on safety, cleanup, and disposal.

Safety Equipment for the Work Area

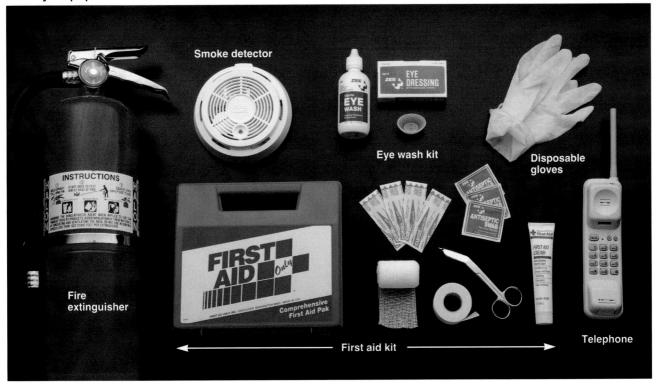

Smoke detector

Eye wash kit

Disposable gloves

INSTRUCTIONS

FIRST AID Only
Comprehensive
First Aid Pak

Fire extinguisher

Telephone

◄─────────── **First aid kit** ───────────►

Basic safety equipment for the work area includes: a fully charged fire extinguisher rated for type A and B fires, a smoke detector, a first aid kit, an eye wash kit, disposable latex gloves, and a telephone for emergency use.

Protective Equipment

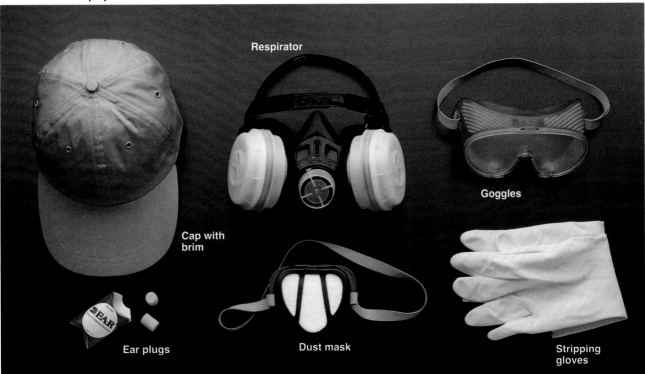

Respirator

Goggles

Cap with brim

Ear plugs

Dust mask

Stripping gloves

Protective equipment for refinishing and cleanup includes: a dust mask and cap with brim, to wear when sanding; a respirator, to wear when using harsh stripping chemicals; goggles and stripping gloves, to wear while stripping and finishing; ear plugs, to wear when operating power tools.

Storage Tips

Hang paint brushes with the bristles down so they dry evenly and completely, and to protect the bristles. If the bristles are bent while the brush is drying, they will become permanently bent.

Label storage containers clearly with a description of the contents and the date the material was first used. Also note any special projects to which a finishing product was applied. NOTE: The best solution to storage issues is to buy only as much material as you need, avoiding leftovers.

Disposal Tip

Guidelines for Working with Chemicals

Leftover paints, strippers, and solvents are considered household hazardous wastes. Wastes produced by stripping and finishing procedures may contain lead, mercury, and other dangerous substances that will pollute landfills and water supplies. Call the EPA Hazardous Waste Hotline at 1-800-424-9346 for information on disposing of these materials responsibly.

•Use water-based strippers, stains, and finishes instead of oil-based products whenever they meet your needs.

•Buy refinishing and finishing materials in the smallest quantity needed for the job, and dispose of leftover materials properly.

•Never pour refinishing or finishing chemicals down the drain.

•At the end of your project, take any unused chemicals to a hazardous waste disposal site, or donate any usable leftover materials to friends or civic organizations.

•Never mix chemicals directly into your household or yard waste without drying first (see *Tip*, left).

Use newspapers and rags to collect residue from finishing. Let the newspapers and rags dry, then throw them out with your household trash. NOTE: Any residue containing lead must be taken to a hazardous waste disposal site.

Cleanup Tips

Wrap wet paint brushes in plastic or foil to store them for up to three or four hours while you wait for a coat of finish to dry.

Reuse mineral spirits. Pour used mineral spirits into a clear container, and allow it to rest until the contaminants settle to the bottom of the container. Pour or siphon the clear mineral spirits into another container for later use. Dispose of the residue properly.

Clean brushes efficiently in a container that is just big enough to hold both the brush and enough solvent to do the job. To ensure compatibility with the solvent, select a container that is made of the same material (usually plastic or metal) as the solvent container.

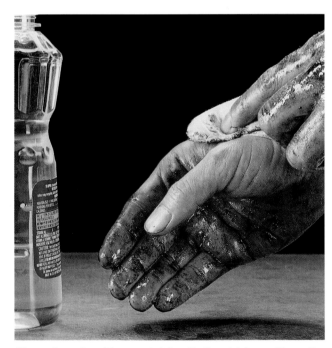

Clean hands with vegetable oil. Scrubbing with ordinary vegetable oil will dissolve and remove most oil-based finishing products. The oily mess it creates is rinsed off easily with soap and water (dish detergent is very effective).

Keep your work area dust free by vacuuming toolboxes, cabinets, woodwork, and light fixtures, as well as all floors and worksurfaces, whenever you complete a sanding project.

Index